SANDI LINDGREN, PHD

I SUPPORT YOUTH!

Success Through the Latest Motivational Approach

POWERED BY

B O O K S

Author: Sandra J. Lindgren, PhD

Title: I SUPPORT YOUth!

ISBN: 978-1-77371-037-2

Category: PSYCHOLOGY/Developmental/Adolescent

Publisher: Black Card Books

Division of Gerry Robert Enterprises Inc.

Suite 214, 5-18 Ringwood Drive

Stouffville, Ontario, Canada, L4A 0N2

International Calling: +1 877 280 8736

www.blackcardbooks.com

....

TESTIMONIALS

"It is Sandi Lindgren's wish to 'help fuel the fire for coaching youth to explode on a global level.' In her new book I SUPPORT YOUth!, *she feeds that fire in a passionate, engaging and practical manner. Sandi is a missionary who educates readers about the value and values of professional coaching and describes how it can be differentiated from the roles of parent, teacher, therapist, mentor, and consultant. She carefully walks readers through the steps needed to become a professional life coach and offers a clearly conceptualized introduction to core knowledge, principles, and methods for her Supportive Youth Coaching Model.* I SUPPORT YOUth! *is chockfull of helpful coaching hints and tips as well as hands-on illustrations that bring youth coaching to life for readers. I highly recommend this book to anyone who is interested in catching the fire and becoming a youth coach or has an interest in seeking a youth coach for oneself or for a young person in one's life."*

—**Andrew Malekoff, MSW**
Executive Director and CEO, North Shore Child
and Family Guidance Center, New York
Author of *Group Work with Adolescents:*
Principles and Practice, 3rd Ed (Guilford Press)
Editor-in-chief of the professional journal, *Social Work with Groups*

TESTIMONIALS

"Sandi is a mission-driven pioneer on the 'coaching for youth' global stage. Her message and practical insights and application are a must read for any coach who shares her passion for helping youth today via coaching. It is also a read for any young person who wants to show up like she did in her own youth—paving the way for what the coaching profession is today. RUN to order a copy of this book!"

—Diana Sterling
Author, *The Parent as Coach Approach*,
2007 (revised)

"Young people face many challenges, not least school, peers, and hormones. Coaching is an excellent tool for helping young people develop a stronger understanding of themselves so that they can explore the consequences of alternative courses of action, helping them develop greater personal responsibility. Sandi's book is an excellent resource for those working with young people and who want to move from a directive to a facilitative style of communication and through that help young people become the best they can be."

—Professor Jonathan Passmore
University of Evora, Portugal

"I SUPPORT YOUth! *is a highly motivating and accessible book for professional coaches who want to encourage and inspire young people. It is well-researched and full of practical ideas and real-life case studies. Highly recommended."*

—David McNally
Bestselling Author of *Mark of an Eagle:
How Your Life Changes the World*

"I SUPPORT YOUth! *is an excellent resource for youth coaches of all nationalities and cultures. It has practical applications that can be adapted to the needs of all children. Helping to identify mental health issues and sharing resources that address these concerns are imperative. We live in a social period that has created distrust, paranoia and even dishonesty.* I SUPPORT YOUth! *creates a foundation that shows the reader how to coach teenagers in a way that works. This book is a must-read for everyone who is working to make a difference in the life of our youth."*

—**Titilayo Bediako, MS EdS**

Founder and Executive Director,

WE WIN Institute

"It is a delight to read such a well-informed and practical guide for those who wish to support young people through the power of coaching. An easy read which is also a step-by-step guide that will help the reader understand the hows and whys of youth coaching. Sandi's knowledge and passion shine through every page and provide a firm foundation from which the reader can build their own youth coaching success stories. A must-read for all those thinking or indeed coaching in this area."

—**David Jessop**

www.phoenix-lifecoaching.co.uk

LIFT International, Academy Award Winner – LIFE Lifter of the Year

Keynote Speaker, Anthony Robbins Global Youth Leadership Summit, San Diego

TESTIMONIALS

"Sandi Lindgren has done youth coaching a great service in giving the field a comprehensive guide to the practice. Sandi's education and vast experience allow her to provide practical answers and client interactions that will enable coaches in this field to excel!"

—**Mark Demos**

Founder, Talent DNA, My Life Scene,

and 321Go.college

"Sandi Lindgren reminds everyone who is committed to promoting the health and well-being of young people that there are best practices and tried and true ways for adults to come alongside these youth. Her lived experience gives significant credibility to the ideas and model presented in this book. If every adult met every young person in the way that Sandi does, our youth would all be better positioned for success, feeling loved and accepted as they are."

—**Carolyn M. Porta, PhD, MPH, RN, SANE-A, FAAN**

Professor and Director, Global Health, School of Nursing,

University of Minnesota

"With passion and fun, Dr. Lindgren illustrates the highs and lows of working with youth. This book will be what current and future staff discerns as their trusted compass in effective youth work leadership. I wish this book had been around when I was starting my career with youth! There's real wisdom in these pages with practical advice that can be applied quickly and easily. If you can figure out how to get this book into the hands of every youth worker, it will spark dedication and passion for the field."

—**Tish Bolger**

CEO, Girl Scouts Minnesota and

Wisconsin River Valleys

"I SUPPORT YOUth! *provides a great framework on how to partner with and support youth in achieving the goals they have for themselves through a coach model of youth work. This model can be incredibly effective in many different settings, including schools, child welfare and juvenile justice systems, mental health facilities and non-profits that are working with youth experiencing crisis such as homelessness. What I appreciate the most about this model of youth work is that it centers the youth as being the one who is developing and setting their own goals (the driver of their own life as it should be) and then the coach helps support and empower them to accomplish these goals."*

—**Beth Holger**

Executive Director, The Link,

Minneapolis, Minnesota

"What could be more meaningful than using the art and science of coaching in supporting the youth, that is, the future generations of this planet? This is exactly what Sandi has been doing for a long time and now she is calling us to learn from her experience and spreading it around the globe. Some people are like lighthouses; their light truly illuminates the world. Sandi is definitely one of them. I strongly recommend you to read this book and answer her noble call to duty."

—**Tuncel Gulsoy**

MCC Executive Coach,

Istanbul, Turkey

TESTIMONIALS

"This book is a must-read for those interested in helping support youth, and in particular, for youth workers. It deals with developmental and ethical issues, provides resources, and highlights skill sets needed to work with youth. Sandi makes use of skillfully asked questions and also brings to light a number of interdisciplinary models. Her approach is deeply compassionate."

—Irv S. Katz, PhD
Chancellor, International University of
Professional Studies

"I SUPPORT YOUth! is bound to be a 'best seller' for professionals looking at ways to reframe, communicate, and motivate youth they serve and support! Sandi provides practical strategies, tips, and insightful ways for adults to engage and inspire youth. Chapters are organized well, easy to follow, and include important focus content on ethical considerations, adolescent development, and emotional intelligence. Already looking forward to book two!"

—Dan Porter, M.S.W., L.I.C.S.W.
Social Worker Supervisor, Professional Development Board Chair for Minnesota School Social Workers Association, Book Reviewer for the
School Social Work Journal

"I SUPPORT YOUth! is a must-read for everyone who works with young people. Dr. Lindgren lays out useful approaches to working in support of all youth. Her easy-to-use tools and clear and practical advice will be an important asset to teachers, social workers, counselors and anyone who works with teenagers."

—Dr. Alan Tuchtenhagen
Director, The Center for Leadership Studies,
Augsburg University

"I SUPPORT YOUth! *is a powerful balance of research, experience, context and practical application. Sandi's ability to clearly identify the unique role of a coach in a team of professional services is the vantage point from which she introduces a fresh and insightful look at the core skills of the job. I have read sound theory in adolescent development, emotional intelligence and motivational engagement from many sources, but this book has been a concise and insightful study of methods to exercise the skills in a meaningful way.* I SUPPORT YOUth! *should be on the shelf or reading device of anyone who works with young adults."*

—**Wes Thomsen**
Senior Content Developer/Project Manager
Hazelden Publishing

"I SUPPORT YOUth! *is a must-read for all youth coaches. Sandi Lindgren's Supportive Youth Coaching Model breaks down the significant areas of training required to understand and effectively provide coaching that meets the needs and the varying emotional maturity levels of youth clients. As a coach trainer and passionate advocate for ethical standards in youth coaching, I appreciated the in-depth discussion on proper coach education and adherence to rigorous ethical guidelines for all youth coaches."*

—**Jodi Sleeper-Triplett, MCC, BCC**
Founder and CEO, JST Coaching & Training
Author of *Empowering Youth with ADHD*

FOREWORD

Sandi Lindgren has compiled a much needed and powerfully impactful book for coaching youth and empowering the next generation of adults to be more prepared for life's ups and downs, challenges and opportunities.

As a psychologist in my early professional days, I loved working with youth to have a chance to be a good influence in their lives for future decision making. Yet young people were usually "sent" to a psychologist and had some serious life challenges and chaos or family dysfunction.

I often called myself a coach (long before the coaching profession had evolved). Many of the young people loved that... it seemed less intimidating and stigmatizing.

Sandi has written in this wonderful book very specific ways and means of coaching youth, becoming a youth coach, understanding distinctions between coaching and counseling (psychotherapy). The acceptance and proliferation of youth coaching could truly impact our next generation of leaders, entrepreneurs, scientists, parents, community leaders, and more. Coaching during the formative years of adolescence and beyond, I believe, is crucial. The human brain is not even fully mature until age 22.

If young people have a coach who is objective and non-judgmental, then the "crises" of youth, such as breakups, physical and emotional changes, loss, family chaos, and identity, will have a safe place for conversations. Then critical thinking, choice making, honest self-reflection, and expression of one's gifts can have a better chance to grow and blossom.

Sandi includes theory and practical application for professionals and also offers tips for parents to be more coach-like with their own children, something that worked in my life with my two daughters in their transition years and adjustment to the divorce of their mom and dad when they were teens.

This book, *I SUPPORT YOUth!*, and its training opportunities should be considered for every school to have coaches available for students, maybe as additional training for licensed counselors. And many parents will find that private youth coaches can be even more objective and helpful outside of the school setting.

Think back to your youth. Could you have not benefited from life coaching? Did you have influential mentors who guided you? Maybe some did, maybe some did not. A coach/mentor should be someone available and accessible to all youth. Coaching is empowering and inspiring because at best, coaches assume the young client is capable, resourceful and creative, and then get them to believe it too.

Having a partner to be your "guide on the side" through life's journey and unexpected events can be a big part of thriving and not just surviving.

—Dr. Patrick Williams
Master Certified Coach, Board Certified Coach, Author, and
"Wise Elder Coach" for four decades

DEDICATION

I dedicate this book to:

- former youth clients, who opened up their hearts to me, and taught me by challenging me to do better.

- youth "in the system," who are most impacted by the strengths and weaknesses of adults who work with them.

- former and current youth-serving co-workers and colleagues, who give their hearts to and go the extra mile for the youth they serve.

- my mom, Joyce E. Lindgren (1934-2016), my biggest writing champion who continues to live in me and influence my work and my life.

ACKNOWLEDGMENTS

Thank you to my amazing support group of girlfriends for continued encouragement and support throughout book writing and all of life's ups and downs. Your patience and non-judgmental support through this eight-year process is a part of why this book is a reality.

As this book is based on my dissertation research, I again give heartfelt thanks to Dr. Carolyn Porta (Garcia) who was instrumental in her guidance and mentorship in academic research and writing.

I couldn't have completed my research without the multitude of youth coaches from around the world who completed my survey, starting with those in the original ICF Teen Special Interest Group.

I want to thank my book coach, Lynne Klippel (LynneKlippel. com), for helping me get out of my academic writing and find my real writing voice.

Thank you to the many folks who generously gave their time, energy and effort to review my book and provide either feedback or endorsements, or both.

Many thanks to Pat Williams, founder of the coach training program (Institute for Life Coach Training) I was first certified in, for answering my challenge to him about including youth coaching with, "Well, why don't you write it then?"

The International Coach Federation for their continued guidance, support and regulation of coaches.

Lastly, thank you to the multitude of youth who have touched my life in ways that I will never forget and provided the motivation for this book.

TABLE OF CONTENTS

INTRODUCTION

*If you work with or want to coach youth,
then this book is for you.*

I'd like you to imagine for a moment yourself at age 16. You decide to seek professional help in making some difficult changes in your life. Imagine yourself sitting in a comfortable room, talking one-on-one with a professional. Perhaps you are talking about some goals or dreams of yours. Maybe these goals or dreams have been eluding you for a while. You are discussing out loud your frustrating roadblocks and experiences, possibly for the first time. You struggled with doubt, lack of self-confidence, and maybe fear. You talk about your parents and their influence on you and your goals and dreams. You could be embarrassed, fearful, or self-conscious as you've not really talked about these details with anyone else. Can you picture it? Can you feel it?

Now imagine having this same conversation with this professional, this time with your parent sitting in the back of the room observing and listening to everything you say. Would it change what you are willing to talk about? Would you change your language, demeanor, or words? Would the presence of your parent listening in affect your conversation with a professional? What if your parent was not actually sitting in the room, but you knew whatever you told the professional would be relayed to your parent?

These two scenarios are part of what brings me to write this book. As a clinical social worker, a therapist, and as a certified professional life coach, I have spent my professional life working to support youth. The goal of this book is to assist you, regardless of your role, to be more effective in your work supporting youth. By supporting you and others, we can affect a greater number of youth to be well supported in their lives.

My Background

I began my lifelong journey as a social worker when I was in high school—where I fielded arguments between siblings, advocated for disability awareness and rights in my school, tried to get along with all of my classmates, and learned first-hand about grief, loss, death, and dying—all before I turned 16 years old. In my 10th grade English class, I wrote the required essay goals about what I saw myself doing in the future and knew then I wanted to be a social worker.

I completed my Bachelor of Arts degree from Concordia College (Moorhead, Minnesota) with a double major in social work and Spanish. My earlier professional career includes time working as an emergency crisis shelter staff, juvenile probation officer, and then leading wilderness trips for court ordered delinquent girls in the north woods of Minnesota. While working there, I completed my master's degree in social work from Augsburg University in Minneapolis and soon after moved there to work at a local Latino mental health clinic.

In early 2000, I became aware of professional life coach training. It sounded too easy, self-fulfilling, and "loosey-goosey," especially because no one could really explain to me what it was. I was concerned about the ethics of coaching while at the same time, I was also feeling frustrated and burnt out with the sense that at times, I was working harder than my clients. There had to be other ways to support and help clients get a clear focus and be motivated by it, not just deal with past pain, but truly be able to move towards their dreams. I chose to pursue more training with the Institute for Life Coach Training[1] (ILCT) as it was created for therapists and counselors who wanted to add life coaching to their skill set.

The simplicity and depth of what life coaching embodied had me hooked. The inside-out approach to coaching, the congruence with my social work training and values, and the non-attachment to outcomes attributed to my interest and growing passion for coaching. In 2004, while working as a school social worker in a local charter school for Latino students, I completed my certification at ILCT. I became certified through the main coaching regulatory organization, the International Coach Federation (ICF) in 2005.

In August of 2006, I joined a small group of youth coaches in what appears to be the very first formal gathering of certified life coaches who were interested in coaching teens. We gathered for conference calls monthly to discuss the nuances of life coaching with teenagers. We found that we agreed upon the importance of coaching teens and young adults, and we developed a support network. Although it was initially sponsored by the ICF, it has since been moved over to LinkedIn, where I currently host it as a closed group. It was through this leadership position that I began to get both more excited and worried about the future of life coaching of teenagers.

As the leader of this group, I fielded questions from all over the country and later the world, related to how to coach teens. The example of the parent sitting in the corner of the room while their teen was being coached is a real example. So is the example of the coach typing up detailed notes of what the youth said and sending it to the parent after each session. I was frustrated and worried by the fact that some coaches didn't feel it necessary to get parental permission to work with kids under the age of 18 or discuss confidentiality. Hearing that some life coaches don't believe they need to tell anyone if their teen client talks about

1   www.lifecoachtraining.com

abuse led me into a panic. I wondered why coaching ethics didn't really address working with youth. I wanted to know if I was an outlier in my thinking, and, if not, I realized we needed to do something for the life coaching industry to educate and teach the basics if those coaches are going to coach teens—and especially minor youth. This is what led me to pursue and complete my PhD in Professional Coaching and Human Development.

I SUPPORT YOUth! Success Through the Latest Motivational Approach is a compilation of my dissertation research and professional experience coaching teens and young adults, with insight from other youth coaches throughout the world. What you'll learn by reading this book is the nuts and bolts of coaching youth and why it is important. I'll describe the "Supportive Youth Coaching Model" that I developed through my professional experiences and dissertation research. Also included are the ages and stages of adolescent development and issues like mental health, ethical considerations, and core competencies (basic skills) for coaching youth. An additional chapter on emotional intelligence and youth shows its importance for the future success of our youth. Interwoven throughout are real life stories (names and identifying factors changed, of course) from my own and other coaches' experiences, quotes from youth-coaching clients, and motivation for you to get started or to increase your effectiveness in supporting youth through life coaching skills.

Although the word "youth" and even "teenagers" can mean various ages, I generally mean between the ages of 13-20 years old with a focus on teens under the age of 18. For those who have received life coach training, this book is written for you, to help support your work in coaching this population. If you are already a social worker, teacher, youth worker, or other professional working with youth and you'd like to learn more about how coaching works to support this age group, this book is for you. If you're a parent of a teen, this book will help you make decisions related to hiring and working with a professional to support your child. And if you are in a position to make funding and hiring choices for youth-serving programs, this book provides you with information to make a case to include life coaching services in your programming.

There are parts of this book that talk about coaches having parental permission to coach minor youth. It's important to note that youth workers and youth-serving organizations that work with homeless, sex-trafficked and LGBTQ+ and youth in foster care are disproportionately youth of color and often are unable to get parental permission for participation in services. These youth-serving organizations, as well as schools, are some of the best avenues for all to have the opportunity to experience life coaching, and already have systems in place which allow for youth to participate in and receive their services. Coaching can be an important way to support youth who are on their own, and are responsible for making big decisions about their lives.

> **The goal of this book is to educate trained coaches on the nuances of working with youth, and to show the world how powerful and transformative life coaching can be for all youth!**

Finally, it is important to note, that by reading this book, you will not be considered a life coach (unless you have already received professional coach training). The goal of this book is to educate trained coaches on the nuances of working with youth, and to show both coaches and non-coaches how powerful and transformative life coaching can be for youth!

Feedback is important in coaching, so please let me know what YOU think.

—Sandi

CHAPTER 1

NUTS AND BOLTS OF COACHING

What Is Life Coaching?

The International Coaching Federation (ICF) defines coaching as "partnering . with clients in a thought-provoking and creative process that inspires them to maximize their personal and professional potential."[2] Professional coaching has some regulation, specific competencies, and expectations, as well as a code of ethics for those belonging to a professional coaching organization. The basics of coaching have been created from multiple professions including psychology, social work, leadership development, adult development and learning styles, communications, personal development, management consulting, and various types of counseling.

2   www.coachfederation.org/about

A coach is a "partner" with the coaching client (coachee) rather than the expert who will help fix the client or get them to a more normal level of functioning. The coaching client is already fully capable and interested in finding solutions rather than healing from pain, trauma, or mental illness. A coaching client has the solution to their problem already; a coach helps them listen to themselves, uncover it, explore it, and truly to find "it".

There is no diagnosis or assessment required in coaching, and currently, it cannot be billed through medical insurance (unless it is related to limited "health coaching"). There are many types of coaching, including corporate or business coaching, personal and professional life coaching, spiritual coaching, health and wellness coaching, and even parent, family, and youth coaching. Although there are many similarities between coaching and therapy, there are also many distinctions that separate them.

Generally, the focus of therapy is to resolve difficulties a client has (often due to an experience in their past) and focuses on increasing the social and emotional functioning of the client so they can deal with the present in healthier ways or return to their normal level of functioning. For those interested, there are already various books and information that exist describing the distinctions between coaching and therapy or psychology.

What Professional Coaching Is NOT

In the context of life coaching, it is important to distinguish what coaching is not. In definitions of coaching youth, these distinctions will become more important, especially in the field of education where the word "coaching" is used in so many formats that almost everyone is confused about what the term means. Coaching is neither deficit-based nor is it any of the following: Therapy, counseling, consulting, training, teaching, supervision, mentoring, educational coaching for academics, or sports coaching. The true essence of coaching does not involve telling anyone what to do or trying to convince someone to do something.

How Does Coaching Work?

There is no one way to coach. However, coaching usually begins with helping the client (individual or organization) to identify and clarify values and

> The true essence of coaching does not involve telling anyone what to do or trying to convince someone to do something.

goals and create a shared vision for the coaching time. Coaching mainly focuses on the present, and coaches use common helping professional skills, such as listening, empathy, clarifying, and asking questions. Coaching has an art form to asking powerful questions that elicit insight for the client. Each meeting or session usually includes some form of goal setting and accountability. There should be a coaching agreement prior to the start of the coaching relationship, and the professional coach should have professional coach training and adhere to a code of ethics they can share with their clients. For those interested, there are many coach training organizations that will teach you what you need to know about coaching. I would recommend starting with the list of ICF accredited training programs.[3]

Background of Coaching

Coaching is an emerging and growing international industry that began to take shape in the early 1990s. It has integrated concepts from multiple disciplines of adult development, including psychology, sociology, psychotherapy, education, communication, management, and leadership. Each year, there is a dramatic increase in the number of coaching schools, organizations and people

3   www.coachfederation.org/icf-credential/find-a-training-program

referring to themselves as coaches. Demand for professional coaching is increasing, as is substantial research demonstrating the effectiveness of coaching efforts.

Professional coaching has been steadily building its research foundation, although most of this has been focused on executive or business coaching. In an effort to establish structure and consistency within the field, an organization called the International Coach Federation (ICF) was founded in 1995. The purpose of the ICF is to give insight into the coaching industry and the standards for a credentialed or certified coach. There are different expectations about coaching related to dual relationships, responsibility issues, ethical guidelines, and the role of supervision in coaching.

The International Coach Federation

The best way for me to describe the background of coaching is to talk about it within the context of the ICF, which was the first and remains the largest global professional coaching association. According to its website,[4] there are currently members in over 100 countries. The ICF documents the growth of professional coaches through its Global Coaching study citing 2,100 in 1999 to 47,500 in 2012, and adds about 2,000 new members per year.[5]

From its inception, an important goal of the ICF has been the regulation of the coaching industry and working to "preserve the integrity of coaching through internationally accepted professional standards," especially through the following resources for coaches:

- Core competencies
- Code of ethics and standards
- Credentialing program

4   www.coachfederation.org
5   www.coachfederation.org/faqs

- Accreditation for coach-specific training programs
- Discussion opportunities through Communities of Practice (formerly called "special interest groups")

The ICF has created and defined the core coaching competencies which form the basis of the professionals' defined skills and abilities. The ICF created a code of ethics for coaches and developed three distinct levels and qualifications of certification for coaches.

To give you an idea of what the most basic level of certification requires, I'll use the ICF's first level of certification as an example. These requirements are: A minimum of 60 hours accredited coach training, 100 hours of client coaching experience, and at least 10 hours working with a qualified mentor coach. Applicants must also pass a performance evaluation (written and oral) demonstrating minimum skill requirements. The organization emphasizes the development of credentialing standards for coaches and accreditation standards for coach training programs. The ICF also provides certification for qualified individuals and accreditation of coach training organizations. In addition, this organization also initiated efforts to support quality research for the coaching industry to contribute to establishing credibility and consistency in coaching practices and preparation. Not all coaches belong to the ICF, and it is important to know that other great coaching organizations also exist and certify qualified coaches, as do individual coach training schools. The ICF core competencies and code of ethics are discussed in more detail in the later chapters.

Coach Training

Do coaches have to be trained? Technically, no, which is a problem. As professional coaching is not regulated like professions, such as social work and psychology, this means *anyone* can be called a coach even if they have no training of any sort. Because the word "coach" has become so common and is used interchangeably with other words, there is much confusion about just what it means. Therefore, if you are going to hire a coach, it is important to check their credentials. Look into professional associations, training, credentials, background, and hear from others who have worked with the coach. Ask a potential coach what his/her training is, where they trained, and how long they have been coaching. A master's degree in social work does not make one a coach; it makes you a social worker with a master's degree. If you plan to invest in coach training, my advice is to be sure to go through an accredited coach training program.

 If you are going to hire a coach, it is essential to check their credentials.

Most coaches receive their training from coach training programs that provide initial and basic foundational training for coaching students. The foundational training is often between 30–60 hours of intensive training on the basic premise and skills of life coaching. Subsequent training programs branch off into specialty certification in specific areas, including health and wellness coaching, spirituality coaching, business and executive coaching, and life coaching. If much of your professional background is in working with youth or teens or young adults (and you enjoy it), your coaching specialty area will most likely be youth coaching.

Common Questions of Youth Coaches

Here are some additional comments and questions that have been asked of me by certified coaches related to training and support for coaching youth:

- *"I have only coached adults and have just been approached by a high school teacher about coaching one of his high school students. This student lives in California and is under 18. Does anyone have any experience or resources that can help me identify what I may need to know about getting this teen to enter in a coaching relationship that is legal and ethical? I would imagine there would need to be parent/guardian approval of some sort, yet my web searching on the matter isn't turning up any answers. Any information you can offer is very much appreciated!"*

- *"Any must-have courses for coaches working with teens and young adults? I am new to coaching and am interested in information or classes to coach this demographic."*

- *"When and how are we supposed to include parents when we coach a teenager? Do we have to get written permission or is verbal OK? Should parents be involved in the sessions?"*

- *"Where can a coach go to get specific information or training related to working with teenagers under 18 years old? I mean, there are a lot of rules and requirements related to abuse reporting and getting parent's permission, but there is no place to find this information."*

- *"I have just completed my coach training and have been blessed with my first client, who is a teenager that is a sports star, and of course I am looking forward to working with more kids and teens. Since I am a new coach, I would like some basic advice and special tips when coaching these age groups. Any tools or resources will be welcomed. Thanks a million!"*

- *"I am working with a teenage client, and there is also a therapist working with this family. This therapist has stated to me that I need to have malpractice insurance. I have never heard anything about being required to have this type of insurance. Does anyone reading this post have any information regarding this?"*

- *"Hey there, wondering if someone has a coaching agreement for minors that they could share... I've been coaching women entrepreneurs for the last five years and am now getting requests to work with teenage girls... I have a coaching agreement, just want to make sure I add what is needed for parents and kids. Thanks in advance!"*

- *"... I am very interested in coaching late teens or young adults on the next steps to take in their lives. Guidance counselors are often overwhelmed, understaffed, and under-sourced to really nurture the gifts of our youth, and I believe coaching can be a way to really help to get folks off to a great start. So I am looking to connect with others who may have worked in this area to share ideas, brainstorm, etc. Who do you know that may be of help to me in my search?"*

Summary

By now, you may realize that there are many definitions of coaching. The ICF is one of the largest international regulatory organizations for coaches. Coach training is essential, as anyone can call themselves a "coach" without any training or certification. Coaching youth and young adults is a growing specialty area for coaching. You may have questions similar to those listed here, or other ones. Jot them down as you continue through the book (and I'd love it if you email me your questions that are not answered). I hope to answer them. Now that we've covered the basics of coaching, its background, what is the ICF and coach training, in the next chapter, will cover why coaching youth is so important.

What is your take-away from this chapter?

What are the implications for your work with youth?

CHAPTER 2

WHY LIFE COACHING YOUTH?

Youth Coaching Is Growing Because It Works!

One of the growing specialty areas of professional coaching is coaching youth. Currently, this specialty is not confined to a definitive age group. For example, there are coaches who specialize in entire generations, such as the Millennials or Gen Y, Gen Z, and Gen Alpha or iGen. Other coaches focus on pre-teen children. Some specialize in coaching adolescents and young adults into their early 20s. For each of these youth coaching areas, there is little in the way of coach training for support and education.

There are, however, some coach training programs that have been created by either individuals or small organizations focusing on coaching youth. The majority of these smaller organizations and training programs appear to have been initiated by coaches who have previous education and experience in working with youth. These coaches come from various backgrounds, including youth leadership and development, education, psychology, and social work. They already possess certain skills and knowledge, which they apply to their coaching education and practice. This combination has yielded some powerful and practical guidelines for coaching youth.

Youth coaching is an emerging specialization for coaches. In 2008 in the U.S., there were no ICF-accredited training programs listed on the ICF website for coaching young adults, teenagers, or children; there were seven such training programs in 2018. However, it is important to note that there are also excellent training programs for youth coaches that are not ICF-accredited, but accredited through other coaching organizations, especially those outside of the United States.

Coaching Youth in Education

The current cutting edge of coaching youth appears to be in the educational setting. This may be due to the fact that schools are the obvious place where large numbers of youth gather for a predictable amount of time. Schools are great environments for influencing the learning habits of youth. Teens often spend more of their waking time in school than they do at home. School is the main environment for adolescent development to play out, it is where kids practice and hone their skills related to peer relationships, communication with others, stress management, and academic achievement.

Many school administrators are willing to have a life coach work with their students as long as it appears to yield value for the student, both in their education and their overall well-being. In fact, many educational institutions have realized that hiring a coach for the students, staff, and administrators can help students succeed.

Coaching can be offered during the school day or during after school organized time within a school building. With economic funding decreases, schools are

Schools are great environments for influencing the learning habits of youth.

generally eager to find cost-effective and efficient ways to positively influence the academic success and well-being of many students. Both individual and group coaching of youth within a school is one way to have that impact.

What makes coaching so distinct from other helping professions? Let's take a look at the experience of a high school student referred for school failure/truancy from various perspectives.

- **Therapist**: Begins by interviewing student and parent about life history, focusing in on details, such as presenting problems, family history, birth and developmental history, strengths and challenges, how long school failure has been an issue, and exploring what might be going on socially and emotionally that might impact school failure. If appropriate, the therapist will present a diagnosis (based on the medical model of the Diagnostic and Statistical Manual of Mental Health Disorders V) and submit this to insurance for payment. A treatment plan will be developed to target the main symptoms and issues that arise from the diagnosis, and the therapy sessions will be focused on improving the teen's mental health capacity, which would support school success. A therapist is the "expert" in the relationship and plays an important role in supporting mental health improvements and healing from past wounds. The goal of therapy is often to bring the client back to a "normal" level of functioning.

- **Teacher**: Primary job is to provide educational learning opportunities to support the student's learning of specific subjects, usually based on the teacher's skill set (e.g., Social Studies, Math, Literature, etc.). The teacher or school staff will often need to intervene with students when they are not doing well in school (academically or behaviorally). They talk with student when student misses school, asking what is going on. They will often work with the student to set goals and sometimes, provide little incentives or rewards for school attendance or academic achievements. Parents are contacted. If attendance does not improve, they will have a parent meeting with student at school with appropriate school staff to discuss lack of attendance and explore reasons. Students may be placed on an improvement plan with parental involvement. If problem persists, a truancy petition is filed with the local county, which may lead to court involvement. Teachers and school staff are crucial to a student's education, and through their support and guidance, they are often the first to recognize students who are struggling, both academically as well as socially and emotionally.

- **Parent**: Parents want their kids to attend school and graduate. They generally buy the student an alarm clock, get them up in the morning, feed them, get them on the bus, and sometimes give them a ride to school. They might remove privileges or discipline the student if problems arise. They might also pay student or provide reward incentives if they improve attendance. Parents sometimes (but not always) are the ones youth go to when they are being bullied or not doing well in school. They often get into power struggles related to the issue and are required to attend if a court of truancy petition is filed. Parents are held responsible if student is under the age of 18. They are legally responsible for students until they turn 18 years of age. Students do better when they have parental support while attending school.

- **Mentor**: Shares with student their own high school experience and struggles. Gives tips on getting up in the morning, how to go to bed earlier, and warns of the problems that might occur if they don't improve their attendance. The mentor might also offer reward time going out to eat if they reach the weekly goals and talk with student from the perspective of "someone who's been through it and knows what is best" position. A mentor might be informal (older friend/relative/neighbor, etc.) or a formal mentor working through an agency and assigned to work with a specific student for a limited time. Students who are connected to a healthy and supportive adult are more likely to experience success in school and elsewhere.

- **Consultant**: Studies the school attendance policies and teaches students about the state laws requiring school attendance. They might examine the home environment, student's behaviors in the evening, and create a plan for student to follow, which might include the route to take to school each morning. They might also make suggestions to the school to revise their attendance or transportation policies (if it is the school that hires them). Then their job is done. Consultants are important experts to examine what is going on and make informed recommendations for improvement.

- **Life Coach**: Listens to the student's desires to either attend or not attend school. Asks them if they need any support in getting to school or staying in school. Will explore student values and ask questions about how those values fit current decisions. If student states they want to drop out of school, the coach will explore that possibility with them to help student map out their future without a high school diploma, if that is what they want. The coach will check in with student as they attend or do not attend school and might ask the student about their experience.

If student has a goal to graduate from high school, a coach will explore with student a plan for attaining that goal and then check in along the way. If a student achieves their goal, the coach may ask if they'd like to continue on with more schooling or devise a plan for something else. The student is the expert in this relationship; the coach's job is to support the student's goals, check in along the way, and help the student listen to their own wisdom.

As a high school social worker, I began to use my coaching skills with students, both individually and in groups (with prior permission from the school and parents). Here is the story of a student I'll call Luis.

It was early morning on a school day, and the school halls were empty except for a few random students or teachers passing as classes had already started. A Latino student, who I'll call Luis, knocked on my office door. I was the school social worker in an inner-city charter school. Luis came in and sat down on my little couch in my office. He looked haggard, glassy-eyed with messed up hair. If I didn't know any better, I might have thought he was high. But I knew better.

Luis was a 17-year-old senior in high school and a dedicated student. He was smart, good-natured, had great communication skills, got along with both students and teachers, and had been working hard the last two years to make up missed school credits in order to graduate in a few months. Luis worked full-time at night, and then came straight to school from work to spend the day studying. What little sleep he got came between the hours of 4:00 p.m. and 9:00 p.m.

This was also when family obligations took up his time. He supported his mother and two younger sisters after his father was deported. He had been struggling lately to get his homework completed and sometimes fell asleep in class.

Luis' dream was to graduate from high school and attend college; he would be the first in his family to graduate from high school. All of us at school were worried about his ability to continue to burn the candle at both ends, and things appeared to be spiraling out of control.

"Can I talk to you?" Luis said.

"Sure," I replied.

"Would you like to talk to me as a social worker or life coach?"

"I'll take the life coach today," he replied. Luis had been in one of my coaching groups at the school and understood the differences between a life coach and a social worker. Then he launched into his issue with, "I wanna drop out of school."

As a coach, my response included, "OK, You want to drop out of school... When do you want to drop out? Today? Next week? What can I do to support you dropping out of school? What will you have once you've successfully dropped out of school? What will that get you that you currently don't have?" From those answers, we looked at practice steps of what he wanted to do, how his actions would support his goals (to continue to support his family), how he would succeed in doing this, and then what he would like to do. This led into his future goals, which he quickly realized that he either had to postpone or change because college required a high school diploma. In re-visiting his goals and his values, we came back to what he really wanted, which was to finish the last few months of school and graduate high school with his classmates.

The problem was he couldn't figure out how to succeed with his current situation and dropping out was the only solution he could find. Dropping out was not something he wanted to do. He just felt he had to. He needed to work full-time to pay the rent.

He needed sleep, and he needed to attend school in order to complete his requirements and graduate. He felt it was a win/lose situation.

Through the coaching process, he decided to talk to his boss, his family, and his teachers in order to see if there were other solutions to be found. If there wasn't another solution to be found in two weeks, he would drop out. Within that time, his boss flexed his working hours so he could have more sleep on school days and make up his hours on the weekends; his teachers flexed on attendance requirements and incorporated some additional project credits, and his family agreed to try to support his need for study and sleep time.

I believe that the coach approach of putting the ownership and responsibility on the client is the key to creating awareness and motivation.

Three and a half months later, Luis graduated from high school and was accepted at a local college.

I realize a school social worker approach may have the same or similar results with this client. However, I believe that the coach approach of putting the ownership and responsibility on the client is the key to creating awareness and motivation. For youth, this experience is such a rarity (that adults expect them to be fully capable and responsible) that it is extremely powerful. The key, I find, is to balance the "capable, responsible, resourceful" tempered with developmentally appropriate questions and expectations for youth while allowing them to explore possible solutions.

As students became familiar with coaching and the difference between my job as a social worker and my role when I was wearing my coach hat, they often requested to talk to me as a coach.

One year, with the support of the school staff and administration I coached the entire group of seniors to support their goal of graduation. I held weekly group coaching sessions for the seniors and offered individual coaching to those who wanted. Here's a feedback from one 18-year-old graduate who came back in the fall after her graduation to say thanks for the coaching:

"Because of life coaching, I now have the skills to set goals on a daily basis. I write them on my calendar. I now make lists every day to work towards my goals and get things done."

Another student who participated in the seniors group said the following:

"I didn't understand why we were spending so much time looking at our dreams and our goals rather than working on our homework, but now I understand why. Coaching taught me that if my dreams are connected to my values, then I have more motivation to reach my goals." (19-year-old student)

And another,

"The group coaching was OK, but I got more out of the individual coaching. I was ready to drop out of school because I was so behind in credits, and I had so many pressures outside of school... but coaching helped me realize that if I stayed with it, I really could graduate." (18-year-old student)

Why Are Coaching Skills Important?

Learning life coaching skills will help you be better at whatever it is you do. It has helped me to become more effective as a social worker, a therapist, a college adjunct faculty, and as a supervisor. I utilize coaching skills in my professional roles when it fits, and I also have my own coaching business where I just coach.

Coaching allows me to get to the heart of an issue much faster. It's as if I have permission to be blunt, to listen even more to what the client wants, and to ask questions that elicit solutions to their very own problems. I don't have to fix anyone. I am better able to connect my clients with their own goals, and thus find my clients have greater motivation in completing their goals. I also have more satisfaction in my work, as I don't find myself working harder than my clients any more. Who doesn't want that?!

As a therapist, I've also used skills from my coaching toolbox. Here's an example of how coaching skills helped me in my role as a therapist.

I was working with a 16-year-old therapy client I'll call Susana. She was diagnosed with both depression and anxiety and had been in and out of in-patient psychiatric hospitals four times in the past year for suicide attempts and self-harm (prior to me seeing her).

In my first intake session with Susana, my coaching skills kicked in. When I asked her to explain why she wanted therapy, her response was, "I don't know... I guess because I keep hurting myself, and I want to die." I asked the appropriate therapeutic questions to ascertain whether her cutting was an attempt to kill herself (the answer was no).

And the coaching question that popped up was, "Well if you *really* want to die, *if that's your real goal*, then what's getting in the way of you succeeding?" And that was enough for Susana to look at me clearly and say, "I don't really want to die. I just don't like my life the way it is." So I said, "So should we set some goals about dying, or should we set some goals about changing how you like your life?" (This was enough of a surprise, using a type of coaching question in this part of the intake to move my client towards what she really wanted.) Susana chose life.

Now, don't get me wrong—this client was **not** a life coaching client. This was a therapy client. However, I used my coaching skills in therapy with this client and found it a helpful approach at various times during our therapy sessions.

Two years later, Susana had no further hospitalizations. She successfully completed intensive therapy (individual and family), graduated from high school, and was attending college. As a therapist, you can add coaching skills to your repertoire to support your therapeutic work.

> If you have any desire to improve your effectiveness in working with youth and supporting their development and achievement, then coaching is for you.

Summary

As reported in my dissertation, there is evidence that youth who participate in life coaching programs experience multiple benefits to their health, social and emotional well-being as well as their academic success (Lindgren, 2011).[6] My research also indicated that youth coaches agree that life coaching is an appropriate process to support youth and does provide them with benefits, which include an increased sense of self, improved relationships, and strengthened life skills.

The Supportive Youth Coaching Model covered in the next two chapters provides timely guidance to life coaches who work with youth. Youth blossom under the coaching experience in a way I have never seen before. I've had teens tell me the following:

6 Researchportal.coachfederation.org/MediaStream/PartialView?documentId=516

- *"No one has ever asked me questions like you have."*

- *"Coaching is like having space to explore things and decisions to see if it's what I really want."*

- *"No one ever asked me what I would do with my life if I knew I would not fail. I surprised myself at my answer!"*

- *"What's really weird is that you never told me what to do... and somehow by listening to me and asking me questions, I was able to listen to my own self and hear what I was saying."*

If you have any desire to improve your effectiveness in working with youth and supporting their development and achievement, then coaching is for you. Now that you've learned some of the distinctions and benefits of learning life coaching skills to support your work with youth, you're ready to move into the Supportive Youth Coaching Model in the next two chapters.

What is your take-away from this chapter?

What are the implications for your work with youth?

CHAPTER 3

A SUPPORTIVE YOUTH COACHING MODEL: KNOWLEDGE AND PRINCIPLES

(PART 1)

In my interactions with other youth coaches from around the world, I found that people who had prior experience working with youth had similar beliefs and values, relative to coaching young people. I also noticed that coaches with no prior education or experience related to youth work often struggled with coaching this population and had differing beliefs and approaches than experienced youth workers. I was interested in learning more about the educational background and training of youth coaches and the extent to which this influenced their style and perceptions of coaching this population. I was also interested in growing a supportive community, where coaches working with youth could ask questions and get answers and support related to coaching this population.

Some of the statements from other youth coaches motivated me to do research, as I knew I wasn't the only coach who had positive experiences and results coaching youth. Some of the statements I didn't agree with included:

- *"Coaching doesn't work for teens; they are too focused on their peers to work on self-development."*

- *"I find that teenagers really are not ready for the experience of coaching. They don't show up for scheduled appointments and lack the necessary follow-through required for successful coaching."*

And one coach even stated:

- *"Teenagers these days are too lazy to appreciate the work required of them in coaching; they come to coaching sessions unprepared and fail to follow through on their homework."*

I began to wonder why some of us found life coaching to work beautifully with teenagers, while other coaches struggled and believed teens were too young to engage in a coaching experience. I also wanted to explore my own beliefs about coaching youth and how they were different or similar to those of other youth coaches. Therefore, this was the topic of my dissertation research.

In order to organize my own thoughts, I took my life experience of working with youth as a social worker, therapist, case manager, group leader, and life coach and created a youth coaching model. This model includes three core elements I believe are important when coaching youth. The theoretical background for this model draws from the coaching industry, related disciplines, including social work and psychology and theories and research on adolescent and positive, youth and leadership development. It also includes approaches, such as cognitive-behavioral, strengths based, solution-focused, and positive psychology.

The overarching purpose of my research was to explore the degree to which youth coaches utilize proposed model components that are significant when coaching youth. For research purposes, I defined "youth" as adolescents between the ages 13-20. For those interested, my full dissertation is available online on my website as well as in the ICF research portal.[7]

Supportive Youth Coaching Model

The Supportive Youth Coaching Model I designed identifies and clarifies important distinctions that set apart coaching youth from adults. This model, called the "Supportive Youth Coaching Model," includes three parts:

1. **Core Knowledge:** The foundational background or training for effective coaching of youth;

2. **Core Principles:** Clear guidelines for the coaching experience; and

3. **Core Methods:** Key aspects of youth coaching.

7   researchportal.coachfederation.org

The uniqueness of this particular coaching model is that it distinctly focuses on what it takes to coach youth (adolescents ages 13–20) with specific parameters for coaching minor youth (under age 18).

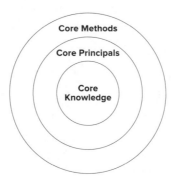

Figure 1. Components of a Model for Coaching Youth

There are subcategories within each of the three core areas of the model as outlined in Figure 2.

Core Knowledge	Core Principles	Core Methods
Coach Training	Culture	Strengthening Self
Adolescent Development Training	Ethics	Increasing Skills
Group Facilitation	Boundaries	Supporting Education
Ethics Training	Logistics	Including Parent
	Agenda	Accessing Resources
		Providing Individual and Group Coaching

Figure 2. Model Subcategories within Each Component

Many individual coaches who currently coach youth have prior professional youth work experience and/or education. Thus, they have individually developed their own youth coaching practices. This model encompasses what I believe to be effective youth coaching practices or factors that support effective practice. I've created position statements for each of the three components as well as for each subcategory to help explain and clarify each section.

Relationship between Components

In the proposed model, the three components are interrelated. The theory behind the model presented is that all three components should be present in order for coaches to be most effective with youth. All the components include aspects of coaching that are either distinct from adults or have a different interpretation due to youths' developmental ages and stages.

First, there is *Core Knowledge* that provides the foundation of what a youth coach needs to effectively coach youth. This includes formal training in and experience with a) life coaching, b) adolescent development, c) group facilitation, and d) ethics. (The ethics here are related to legal obligations related to coaching minor youth.) Lack of core knowledge may negatively impact the core principles.

The second component in the model is *Core Principles*. These core principles guide the coaching agreement and are influenced by the core knowledge. The core principles include aspects of the coaching agreement that might be different than agreements with adults based on youth's age and lifestyle. This includes a) culture, b) ethics, c) boundaries, d) logistics and e) agenda.

> **The theory behind the model presented is that all three components should be present in order for coaches to be most effective with youth.**

The third component of the model is *Core Methods*. These core methods are often the heart of youth coaching and the focus of where time is spent in coaching sessions with youth. I am not purporting that a coach needs to provide each of these core methods. I am suggesting that by being knowledgeable in these common issues faced by youth, a coach can increase the success of the coaching experience with youth. Lack of core knowledge and principles can negatively impact the actual coaching interaction with youth. Core methods include a) strengthening self, b) increasing skills, c) supporting education, d) including parents, e) accessing resources, and f) providing both individual and group coaching. Core knowledge informs both the core principles and the core methods. The core principles inform the core methods.

Someone coaching youth might take the core methods, add some methods of their own or remove some. The result might be successful with coaching youth or not (to the detriment of the youth). Without the core principles, one might miss out on some important instructions needed to be successful, and one might miss some crucial elements that youth need. Being mindful of the ethics and boundaries around working with youth and talking about them with youth and their parents/guardians can lead to a more successful working relationship. Success in youth work is often influenced by building trust within the relationship. Building trust can be supported through setting clear expectations and sharing information prior to coaching. Successful youth coaching includes understanding youth and their culture. Without the foundational core knowledge, the richness of the experience in coaching youth can be lost as well as the benefit for the youth.

Next, we'll go through each of the three core sections along with the subcategories in each area. Don't be confused by ethics being mentioned in two categories. It came up enough in my research that it needed to be included in two different areas. I'll explain the differences below. Also, for the sake of clarifying and helping order, below I have numbered the three categories (1, 2, 3) and the subcategories (a, b, c). As a part of my research, I created a position statement in italics to help guide the reader. If time is short in reading this section, just read the position statements in italics under each heading.

1. Core Knowledge

In order to be effective, youth coaches need to be trained in and knowledgeable about coaching, adolescent development, group facilitation (if they are to do groups), and ethics related to working with minor youth. This first component includes each of the following areas: Coaching training, adolescent development, group facilitation (if applicable), and ethics training.

1a. Coach training. *Youth coaches need foundational knowledge of life coaching and of the industry and its practices prior to coaching youth.* The first aspect of the training recommends those who coach youth complete basic coach training consisting of a *minimum* of 60 educational hours (more is better). This is the number currently required for an ICF basic coach certification level. The second aspect of coach training is that the educational offering is accredited or certified by either the ICF or another similar coaching organization.

1b. Adolescent development training. *Youth coaches need knowledge of adolescent development either from education or experience.* Due to their age, youth have issues related to their development and lack of experience in the world. It is important for coaches to understand adolescent developmental stages and issues that are unique to this age group. A *minimum* of eight hours of training in adolescent development is recommended. Youth coaches need to understand how to adapt their general coaching specifically to youth based on developmental issues and differences related to gender, ethnicity, ability, identity, socio-economic status, and other factors. The importance of adolescent development knowledge lies in the fundamental ability to understand and therefore effectively work with youth.

1c. Group facilitation training. *Youth coaches need training in group facilitation. This, along with training in adolescent development and coaching, assists them in understanding how to facilitate youth coaching groups.* Many, but not all, youth coaches provide group coaching experiences for youth. With a skilled group coach facilitator, group coaching can be a positive experience youth can benefit from and enjoy with their peers. Developmentally, youth are more focused on and influenced by their peers than adults. Because many coaches connect with youth in school settings, group coaching is often an acceptable and encouraged way for coaches to work with youth in schools. It is important for coaches, who are going to facilitate group coaching with youth to understand group facilitation processes. Even the most experienced group facilitator can benefit from support via peer critique or supervision (e.g., peer supervision or consultation) of their group experiences.

1d. Ethics training. *Youth coaches need information and training about ethics related to minor youth. This information should include any aspects pertinent to legal obligations the coach may be required to adhere to when working with youth.* These obligations may change depending on the region or country in which the coach is working. Youth can be considered vulnerable and often are protected by law differently than adults. Coaches should have ethics training that includes issues specifically related to working with youth under the age of 18, such as the age of consent or the reporting of suspected abuse. Although coaching is a "partnership" it is important to note that when coaching youth, the coach will have more "power" in the relationship, which is why we will talk more in depth about boundaries. This knowledge will strengthen the coach's ability to clearly set boundaries and agreements with youth prior to beginning the coaching.

Let's take an example of the 17-year-old student Luis from Chapter 2. A trained life coaching *without* core knowledge of adolescent development might assume that Luis had the ability and foresight to connect his lack of sleep to difficulty in concentrating on his homework, or that he had the ability to problem solve his situation and follow through with a plan to graduate. Ethics for coaching Luis included my having parental permission to coach him. We also discussed issues that he needed to gain parental permission about prior to making a decision.

Ethics is listed again in the second area of the Supportive Coaching Model core principles. The previous example of coaching Luis is illustrative. Ethical considerations for coaching Luis would be to consider his cultural and family expectations as a part of the problem-solving as well as the solution. As Luis' family relied on his salary for their rent and living expenses, it would have been culturally disrespectful and unrealistic to suggest as an option for him to stop working until he graduated from high school.

2. Core Principles

Youth coaches have additional guidelines to follow and clarify in the agreement stage, especially with minor youth. These include ethical considerations, maintaining clear boundaries, and considering various logistics of the actual coaching. These principles help to distinguish the difference in creating and maintaining ethical guidelines between coaching adults and coaching youth and making adjustments for the developmental issues commonly associated with adolescence.

2a. Culture. *Youth coaches must consider and support a client's culture (race, gender orientation, sexual orientation, ethnicity, religion, ability, social and economic, language and national origin, etc.) in all aspects of their work with that client.* It is the coach's responsibility to raise awareness and, with permission, open dialogue with client to create a safe and supportive space for the coaching experience. This may include assisting the client in finding another coach, who may share same/similar culture as the client. Although the aspect of culture is just as important for coaching adults, it needs to be included here, as culture is often overlooked for adolescents—especially when services are provided by dominant culture white professionals.

2b. Ethics. *Youth coaches need clear ethical guidelines to follow that are in addition to the general coaching code of ethics provided for adults.* Professionals in the U.S. are expected to have parental permission in order to work with minor youth. This permission is to come from the legal parent or guardian and usually is in writing. Coaches holding other professional licensures must also adhere to those guidelines and related ethical standards (i.e., *duty to warn* and *mandatory reporting* laws). In some states, such as Minnesota, these two *duties* are required for any professional who works with minor youth. There may be a difference in these guidelines not only between countries, but also between states within the U.S.

Depending on the age of youth, parents or guardians *may* be involved in the coaching process or the engagement of the coach. Parents and youth must be given clear information on confidentiality, in writing and verbally, including specifically clarifying what the coach will and will not share with the parent.

As a safeguard to protect minor youth, the U.S. adults who work with minor youth are required to complete a background check performed by the Bureau of Criminal Apprehension (BCA). Background checks are required prior to the start of employment for various professionals working directly with minors. Life coaches in the U.S. working with minor youth should consider having an annual background check performed by an outside agency. Coaches in the U.S. who hire other coaches or organize volunteers to work with minor youth must have background checks completed on those individuals as well.

The code of ethics for life coaching was initially developed by the ICF and approved by the ICF board of directors in 2008. Each coach certified through the ICF is expected to adopt and follow this code of ethics.[8] We will be discussing various aspects of the ICF code of ethics further in Chapter 7. Various coaching organizations have a code of ethics for coaches to follow, as do many coach training organizations. Coaches who are licensed clinicians have an ethical duty to first follow their licensure code of ethics, and secondly, any additional code of ethics, such as that from a coaching association.

2c. Boundaries. *Youth coaches need to create and maintain clear boundaries while coaching adolescents.* It is the responsibility of the coach to clarify and maintain healthy boundaries. Delineation of roles and responsibilities is essential for coaching youth. Example boundary areas to clarify could include money, coach's personal information, communication patterns and mechanisms, confidentiality, roles and responsibilities, and expectations.

8   www.coachfederation.org/code-of-ethics

Coaches should not overly disclose to youth clients in a way that puts the youth into a caretaking role or puts the attention on the adult instead of the youth. Advanced clarification of acceptable communication and frequency will also be important when setting boundaries with youth (e.g., frequency of communication by text or phone).

Coaches should make clear distinctions between counseling and coaching. These distinctions need to be made in language the youth can understand. Also, it is the coach's responsibility to maintain these boundaries with the parent, as well as school staff or other caring and interested professionals working with that youth.

> It is the responsibility of the coach to clarify and maintain healthy boundaries.

2d. Logistics. *Youth coaches need to have different considerations for the logistics for coaching youth in order to be successful. Logistics include how youth arrive to and get home from their coaching sessions—offering a variety of technical variance, including more flexibility in scheduling and being willing to adapt one's coaching style to fit the developmental needs of youth.* Depending on their age and development, coaches need to pay attention to additional logistics when coaching youth that might not be required of them when coaching adults. This could include physical logistics and/or transportation to support the coaching session, such as location and venue or logistics that encourage ease of conducting a coaching session, such as in person rather than telephone coaching or adapting the length of time for a session. Further considerations can optimize coaching youth experiences incorporating knowledge of social networking and other technology (e.g., being tech savvy).

2e. Agenda. *Youth coaches may have an agenda to target specific issues. Someone other than the youth who wants them to target specific issues may hire the coach. Coaches need to be transparent and clarify any agenda prior to beginning coaching.* Coach training makes it clear that coaches should not formulate their own agenda for a client. Any agenda used in the coaching process should be based on the client's priorities and goals. This is also true when coaching youth. Youth coaches are commonly hired by a third party (e.g., the school or other non-profits) to work with youth on a specific target area. This, in itself, would constitute a coaching agenda. The coach's agenda, if any, needs to be transparent to the youth and can typically be specifically verbalized. An example could be, "I am coaching you for the purpose of dropout prevention." The ICF's core competencies require the coach to attend to the coaching client and the client's agenda rather than the coach's agenda for that client. Transparency is key to building relationships, and relationships are the cornerstone of coaching.

When coaching 16-year-old Olga, it was my responsibility as a coach to obtain prior permission from her parent to engage in the coaching relationship. As a part of my intake procedure, I met with Olga and her parent (single mother) prior to the start of coaching. It is during this first intake meeting that I require of potential coaching clients who are minors that I clearly explain the parameters of coaching, the coaching relationship, what coaching is and what it is not, the differences between coaching and therapy, how confidentiality fits in, and what I will and will not share with the parents. I talk about mandatory reporting, duty to warn, communication during the coaching and if we are meeting in person, and how the client will get to the coaching sessions. It is also during this meeting that I, as the coach, get to determine if this is an appropriate coaching client for me, and the client also can determine if they'd like to work with me. We create a mutual agreement of informed consent for the coaching. I have both client (minor youth) and parent sign the agreement prior to the start of coaching. Olga was a client who did not have any obvious mental health issues but was having some common yet potentially serious difficulties. We agreed that coaching would be appropriate for Olga. If it were not (as has happened in other cases), I would refer the client to either a) another coach who might be a more appropriate fit, b) a therapist (if that would be more suitable to the situation), or c) hold off on the coaching until the client was ready. The latter happens most frequently when the parents would like their child's behavior to change, but the child does not want to change the behavior.

Summary

In review, this chapter covered the first two parts of the Supportive Youth Coaching Model made up of core knowledge (training needed) and core principles (guidelines for coaching minor youth). The third (and final) part of this model is core methods, which is covered in the next chapter.

What is your take-away from this chapter?

What are the implications for your work with youth?

A GOAL
WITHOUT A PLAN
IS JUST A WISH

CHAPTER 4

A SUPPORTIVE YOUTH COACHING MODEL: METHODS

(PART 2)

In the previous chapter, The Supportive Youth Coaching Model was introduced. Details of the first two sections, 1) core knowledge and 2) core principles, were covered. This chapter completes the model with core methods, which is the most fluid and flexible of the three components of the model.

3. Core Methods

Youth coaches often encounter common areas of focus for youth, which address specific developmentally important objectives. Core methods include key aspects that coaches *might* focus on when coaching youth. All of these are not necessarily included in all coaching experiences with youth. The coach and youth can together decide what is most beneficial to the youth being coached. With knowledge about adolescent development and the physical, cognitive and social-emotional changes youth experience, coaches can better understand their behavior and more optimally coach youth. The areas listed below were the themes that surfaced in my research. I've expanded on a few of them.

Youth benefit from learning and practicing the process of breaking goals into smaller, more quickly achievable steps.

3a. Strengthening self. *As youth are continually developing their identity, they benefit greatly from coaches who assist them in becoming more self-aware.* This often includes values and strengths identification as well as exploration of their developmental assets. Becoming more self-aware assists youth in developing self-confidence to take steps towards their goals and dreams. This process differs from adults because youth are continually trying on new identities in order to see what fits best for them. They may, for the first time, consider an identity that differs from the one with which they were raised.

3b. Increasing skills. *Youth often want to focus on specific social or life skills that they have not yet mastered.* Although there are varying definitions of each, social skills, emotional skills, and life skills are often used interchangeably when working with youth. Youth are learning basic skills that will assist them in being successful in life and with others. These skills include but are not limited to goal setting, time management, communication, decision-making, and relationship building. I've included a separate chapter on emotional intelligence and youth as these are such key skills to develop. Below, I'll expand on goal setting as it is a cornerstone of life coaching.

Goal setting is considered a fundamental part of the coaching experience. Goal setting with youth often involves not only the teaching of how to set attainable goals, but more frequent check in or feedback with shorter-termed goals. Youth benefit from learning and practicing the process of breaking goals into smaller, more quickly achievable steps. It might be easy to say, "I want to graduate from high school" or "I want to get better grades." It is much more difficult for a youth to figure out the steps that are needed in order for that to happen, and in what order to prioritize them. Developmentally, the executive functioning part of their brain is not fully developed. They often become overwhelmed with all there is to do when looking at the steps needed to achieve their goal. Youth (depending on their age) may also struggle setting long-term goals. Setting short-term goals while knowing their longer-term goal can help youth to experience success and stay motivated. A youth may realize that school attendance affects their grades, but the goal of attending school daily for a year can be overwhelming. Instead, shorter goals with frequent check-ins may provide more motivation. "I'll arrive at school by 8:30 a.m. every day this week and attend all my classes," may be more appropriate. However, if that youth is currently attending school once a week, then even that goal may be overwhelming and unmotivating. Some youth might need frequent check-ins about their goals and a week may be too much time between check-ins for some.

S.M.A.R.T. – V.I.E.W. Goal Setting

Although goal setting is a cornerstone for adult coaching, many youth have not yet learned how to set attainable goals, and often need extra support with goal setting. School staff (as well as other youth workers) continually struggle to teach students how to set and achieve their goals. As a coach, it is crucial that the youth choose their own goals (not the coach, or even their parent choosing the goal for them). In goal setting, SMART is an acronym that is often used to teach goal setting in schools. Although there are differing variations (one quick check on Google reveals multiple variations) of the meaning, SMART generally stands for (S)pecific, (M)easurable, (A)chievable, (R)ealistic, and (T)ime limited. In my own coaching practice, I've added to the SMART acronym and created what I call "SMART-VIEW" goal setting. (You can find a free downloadable worksheet on my website: www.sandilindgren. com.) I've found that adding the VIEW provides further motivation as well as success in achieving that goal. VIEW stands for this: (V)alues, (I)mportance, (E)valuate, and (W)ho? Each one of these comes with questions you can ask to help someone further explore a goal.

V = Values. The question to ask is, "What values of yours are being met by you accomplishing this goal?" Connecting a person's goals to their values increases the likelihood of follow-through. Additionally, it is also possible to connect a person to which values of theirs are not currently being honored (which can also be a self-motivating factor).

I = Importance. The question to ask is, "On a scale of 1-10 (with 10 being highest) how important is it for you to accomplish this goal?" If the score is less than a seven, you can ask further questions to help clarify if this is an appropriate goal at this time. "What would bring this number up to an eight or nine?" might help uncover any hidden agendas for this goal (perhaps it is a parental wish rather than the youth's goal).

E = Evaluate. It's important to stop along the way to evaluate your goals, especially when they are more long-term goals. Sometimes we have goals that are extremely important to us and then either we change or circumstances change; those goals are no longer appropriate. Kids need to learn that it is not only OK, but important to continually re-evaluate their goals and plans for themselves, to check in to see if it still fits, if it is still important, and if it is still a valid goal for them. Youth who do not take the time to re-evaluate goals have been found graduating with a four-year degree and thousands of dollars in debt, only to have a degree in a field they are no longer interested in or enjoy.

Finally, the **W = Who?** "Who will support you with this goal? Who in your life can help you with aspects of this goal setting?" This could be parent(s) who will check in with you about it, a teacher who might spend extra time after school with you, a mentor who might introduce you to others having similar goals, etc. One of the keys to goal setting is to understand that with support, goals are more likely to be accomplished.

The most important part of goal setting is that there is some forward movement and some kind of action the client can take in between sessions. The best goals are simple and make the most sense to the client developmentally. Don't get carried away with huge goals.

3c. Supporting education. *Youth coaches may need to focus on supporting educational success and career planning as a part of the coaching process.* Most youth who receive coaching are in school. Educational success, including what might be getting in the way of success is often chosen by youth as an area of coaching focus. For others, supporting the learning of specific life skills might assist in promoting their educational success without directly focusing on education; this could be an important strategy for youth who have had negative academic experiences and find it difficult to initially identify or set goals related to education.

3d. Including parent. *Youth coaches need clear guidelines related to the involvement of parents in youth coaching. Minor youth often live at home and have parents or guardians who want to be involved in the coaching.* As described earlier, it is crucial for coaches to set and maintain clear boundaries about confidentiality with a parent, regardless of the age of the youth. Parents often pay for the coaching of youth, even when the youth is not living at home. The success of youth coaching can sometimes be dependent on how the coach handles the communication and involvement of the parents or guardians. The client is the youth, not the parent. However, it is important to figure out how to include parents so that they can also support your client in their goals.

3e. Accessing resources. *Youth are in need of resources and often have little experience in finding or knowing how to access them.* Youth often need someone to teach or show them how to access community resources, as well as how to practically contact them. Although the Internet is full of resources, youth often lack experience or understanding about how to seek out other adults as resources. Some youth still struggle with how to leave an appropriate telephone message. Introducing youth to other adults can be a healthy and informative way of helping youth access resources.

3f. Providing individual and group coaching. *Youth coaches may want to offer group as well as individual coaching opportunities for youth.* Developmentally, youth like to spend time with their peers and often prefer to participate in groups instead of individually when given the choice. Group coaching can be more economical for agencies or schools that might consider hiring a coach. Schools are often looking for group opportunities for their students and might be more open to professionals coming into the school who can provide group experiences.

Let's revisit 16-year-old Olga. Her mom wanted her to participate in coaching as her grades had taken a downward spiral in the past year (10th grade), and she was at a crucial point, where if she didn't pass all her classes, the time of her graduation could be affected. Olga was crabby at home and refused to participate in family activities. Olga agreed to coaching only after she found out that she, rather than her mom, could set her goals. She ended up setting goals related to school (passing her math class), friends (spending more time with her friends), and home (improving her relationship with her mother). She agreed to share the overall goals with her parent, but worded the last goal as "improving communication at home" as she didn't want her mom to know she was the target of a goal. We spent three months coaching. Our coaching sessions were conducted at a coffee shop, on the phone, on walks and via text messages. We included her mom to support her smaller, related goals to increase her likelihood of success (working with a math tutor and earning privileges to spend time with friends). Olga's work on improving her relationship with her mother began with her saying "good morning" and "good night" and other general greetings. She found a way to connect with her mother in a non-threatening manner related to cooking. So, she began to ask her mom to teach her to cook specific family recipes. In this way, mother and daughter began to increase the quality time spent together without arguing. Olga realized that by keeping her room clean and doing her chores, she was allowed to spend more time with her friends, and there was less arguing in the house. At the end of three months, Olga was ready to continue her progress on her own. Six months later, she completed her junior year with all her credits and earned an A in math. The following year, she graduated from high school and started college.

Laser Coaching

One more example on the beauty of coaching teens. I was volunteering in the same high school I had previously worked in as a social worker. I offered what I called "laser coaching" during specific coaching office hours. These were short 12–15-minute coaching sessions for students– fast paced, and goal specific. After clearing the way related to permissions and space, I began by offering a 10-minute explanation to the classrooms and informed students where to sign up. The rules were simple. My coaching hours were blocked off in 15-minute increments: 1. Attendance for students had to be voluntary (teachers could not require participation) and 2. Students had to come with a current issue, a goal or a problem that they wanted to address. I met with and coached the students anywhere between 8–15 minutes. Sometimes, they returned the next week or two (or a month later), and sometimes they did not. Issues presented ran from relationship problems, academic struggles, drug addiction, family stress, gang involvement, child abuse, pregnancy, and self-confidence issues, to name a few.

I met with a 15-year-old boy I'll call Tony for a total of 12 minutes. He had been smoking marijuana for the past two years and realized it was becoming a problem; he wanted to quit but didn't dare tell anyone. Most of his friends smoked as well as family members. Within these 12 minutes, I asked questions, listened and repeated back to him the statements he made. He gave me his background, set a plan for how he would quit and who would support him in school and out. He stated that he may or may not come back, but that if he saw me, a "thumbs up" would mean he was drug-free. Tony never returned for another coaching session. However, throughout the next three months, I saw him in the hallway most weeks I was in the school for my coaching office hours. And each time he saw me, he secretly gave me the thumbs up signal.

Summary

The Supportive Youth Coaching Model is comprised of three categories (knowledge, principles, and methods), and each of those has subcategories. The model's purpose is to inform and guide the work of both individuals and coach training organizations in the delivery of appropriate and quality youth coaching. The model is written in broad categories to use as a framework for individuals or organizations to create individualized programming or training to meet their specific needs. Awareness of adolescent development will help coaches avoid some common mistakes in youth work. The next chapter will explore some of the developmental differences in youth in each of the three different stages of development: early, middle, and late adolescence.

What is your take-away from this chapter?

What are the implications for your work with youth?

CHAPTER 5

AGES & STAGES OF ADOLESCENT DEVELOPMENT

Adolescent development is the key to understanding and working effectively with youth. It is the responsibility of professional coaches, who work with youth, to have a clear understanding of developmental needs and issues. Coaches then adapt their work to fit the developmental needs of their youth clients. Ignoring developmental needs would be unprofessional and potentially unethical, opening the door for potential risk on the part of both the youth client and the coach. Children pass through various stages to take specific steps as they transition from childhood to adulthood. The actual stages and ages for the stages differ, and children do not pass through each stage and learn the same skills or experience the stage the same. Development is entirely individual; however, having general developmental knowledge of adolescent stages can help adults support them in a more effective manner. This chapter is related to the core knowledge section of the Supportive Youth Coaching Model. Within each stage, I've outlined the following categories in order to help streamline the information: Physical, social/emotional, thinking/learning (cognitive), and morals/values/autonomy. I've summarized a variety of sources on adolescent development including my favorite publication called "Teen Years Explained"[9] as well as the following organizations that have listed information on adolescent development.

www.childrensmn.org/for-health-professionals/education

www.cyh.com/HealthTopics/HealthTopicDetails.
aspx?p=114&np=122&id=1628

www.cdc.gov/ncbddd/childdevelopment/positiveparenting/
adolescence2.html

www.medlineplus.gov/teendevelopment.html

www.childdevelopmentinfo.com/child-development/piaget/#.
XPwsSS3Mwn0

www.adolescenthealth.org/Training-and-CME/Adolescent-
Medicine-Resident-Curriculum/Adolescent-Medicine-Resident-
Curriculum.aspx

www.aacap.org/Mobile1/Families_and_Youth/Fact_for_Family_
Mobile.aspx

---

9   McNeely, C and Blanchard, J., *The Teen Years Explained: A Guide to Healthy Adolescent Development* (2009), John Hopkins Bloomberg School of Public Health, Center for Adolescent Health, pp. 14-15.

www.oregon.gov/oha/ph/HealthyPeopleFamilies/Youth/
AdolescentGrowthDevelopment/Documents/adoldevstages.pdf

www.16thcircuit.org/Data/Sites/1/media/family_court/Documents/
fff_normal.pdf

www.csmh.umaryland.edu

www.ext.vt.edu/family/child-development.html

I've included in this chapter and within each developmental stage coaching tips that can be utilized by coaches when working directly with youth. At the end of this chapter, I've included some coaching tips for parents in each of the three stages of adolescence.

11–14 years old = Early Adolescence
(Middle School and Early High School)

Early adolescence is a time of many changes for youth (physical, mental, emotional, and social). As their body changes are most drastic during this stage, youth are often worried about body changes and how others look at them, as well as how they compare themselves to others. This is a time when peer pressure begins related to tobacco, drugs, alcohol, and sex. Teens begin to make more of their own choices about friends, sports, studying, and school. It is common for frequent changing relationships, worries about being normal, and of course, there is increased interest in sex. Youth at this stage become more independent with personalities and interests. Parents are still very important, although this is also when youth begin to push back and take risks. Their adult relationships and adults around them help youth formulate their own ideas of whether or not they are looking forward to growing up, which in turn, can impact their choices.

Early Adolescence Traits

Physical

- Both boys and girls have rapidly changing bodies at this stage. Their brains are developing, and they have related hormonal changes that create changes that are visible to others.

Social/Emotional

- At this time, a sense of identity is developing. The visible physical changes often create some concern about body image, looks, clothing, and comparing themselves to peers. At this stage, it is normal for youth to focus on themselves and appear self-centered. It is common for moods and emotions to fluctuate; high expectations and a lack of self-confidence is typical. Most are interested in the present with limited thoughts for their future. Intellectual interests are expanded.

- Peers serve a developmental purpose; there is more interest and influence by peers. It is common to have intense relationships with same-sex friends and have contact with the opposite sex in groups. They may have short-term relationships.

- Youth at this stage are starting to develop their independence and their own value system. They may express less affection towards their parents, think they are all "grown up", and challenge authority. A desire for privacy is normal. Youth at this stage tend to express themselves by actions rather than words.

- Girls tend to focus on WHO they are with and tend to experience more difficulty with depression and anxiety. Boys tend to focus on WHAT they are doing. Social relationships may be unsettling. They tend to be more competitive, and social position can be an issue.

Thinking/Learning

- Early adolescents begin to have more ability for complex thought, although cause-effect relationships are underdeveloped. Concrete thought dominates and vocational goals change frequently.

- Youth at this stage are better able to express feelings through talking and develop a stronger sense of right and wrong, although they may be less socially aware. They start to take into account the bigger picture and begin to develop capacity to reason.

Morals/Values/Autonomy

- Early adolescents often increase testing of rules and limits, experiment with sex and/or drugs and increase questioning of rights and privileges.

- Capacity for abstract thought develops, and they start selecting role models.

- Youth at this stage typically identify with faith or spirituality of family in which they were raised. As they begin to question their own identity and beliefs, their beliefs may also change.

Coaching Tips for Working with Early Adolescents

It is your professional and ethical responsibility to educate yourself and understand normal development so you can help your youth clients (and their parents) prepare for the changes to come in the youth you are coaching. Being familiar with adolescent development will help you as a coach to have developmentally appropriate communication and expectations of the youth you coach. Answer their questions honestly and directly. Youth begin to challenge authority, yet they also

Being familiar with adolescent development will help you as a coach to have developmentally appropriate communication and expectations of the youth you coach.

really want to know what you think. Occasional rudeness is normal, as are complaints that parents are interfering with their independence. When youth this age is stressed out, they will often revert to more childish behaviors.

Talk about peer pressure and encourage them to express their opinions and ask questions (without judgment). These youth have not yet developed their values and identity, and so a values identification exercise may not yet be appropriate. However, this conversation could be introduced in a way that helps them begin to consider the definition of values and also examine familial and cultural values from their family or upbringing and help them to see how they fit. At this stage, youth are more focused on the present and may have difficulty with future visioning activities or goal setting related to their future, so focus goal-related conversations towards more short-term goals and the immediate future (e.g., next week).

Ask questions to encourage conversations about safety (wearing seatbelts, helmets, dangers of drinking, drugs, smoking, and risky sexual activities). During these conversations, ask youth what they think about these topics and spend time listening (without judgment). Youth this age is developing their ability for abstract and complex thought and so are often experimenting with different ideas. Give reminders for coaching appointments and when possible, set up a system where a responsible adult can help remind them as well. If your coaching is in person, make sure the youth has transportation to the coaching site. If on the phone, consider initiating the call rather than waiting for the youth to call. When possible, use texting between coaching sessions to support learning and reminders.

15–18 years old = Middle Adolescence (Late High School)

Middle adolescent years are what most of us think of when we hear the word "adolescent." This is a time when teens change how they think, feel, and interact with others. They are developing a unique personality and their own opinions. As youth age, they will have a clearer sense of self. This is an important time for independence and responsibility; at this stage youth often begin to work. In the United States, many leave their homes after high school. At this stage, their brain development is incomplete (especially in the area of the prefrontal cortex), so some youth are inconsistent in controlling emotions, impulses, and judgments.

Middle Adolescence Traits

Physical

- Girls at this stage reach full physical development and sometimes go through rapid gains in height and weight. Girls who are struggling with body image and emotional issues may be prone to develop disordered eating. Boys come close to reaching full physical development, and their eating habits may change and become sporadic. Both boys and girls need more sleep.

Social/Emotional

- Middle adolescent youth have a clearer sense of identity along with increased emotional stability. Along with this, they are generally more independent and self-reliant, yet at the same time have increased self-consciousness. Still self-absorbed, they may fluctuate between high expectations for themselves and poor self-concept. At this stage, youth can usually think things through (abstract thought) and have increased ability to delay gratification.

- Early or late maturation can create additional stress. For boys who experience early maturation, adults may assume they are able to take on increased responsibility (when they are not yet able). Early maturing girls are more likely to be a target for sexual harassment and/or become involved in dating relationships with older boys before they are emotionally ready. Rapid weight gain and/or emotional struggles may put girls at risk for disordered eating.

- There is less conflict with parents, although they still might be embarrassed to be with them in public. It is common for the youth to feel awkward about demonstrating affection to the opposite sex parent.

- Peer relationships remain important and take appropriate place among other interests. It is common to form strong lasting peer alliances/friendships, engage in fad behaviors, and become cause-oriented. Popularity may be important. Youth at this age often experiment with friends, sex, substance use/abuse, jobs, and risk-taking.

- Increased ability for caring and sharing and developing more intimate relationships. They are more comfortable with sexuality and in dating (not just the opposite sex). Feelings are strong, especially that of love, passion, sadness, or depression.

Thinking/Learning/Cognitive

- Youth in middle adolescence are developing their ability to think ideas through and experience growth in abstract thought and advanced reasoning skills. Cause/effect relationships are better understood, and they have a greater capacity for setting goals. They have a better grasp of irony and sarcasm, although they often revert to concrete thought when under stress.

- These youth are learning work habits and generally show more concern for school and future plans. More importance is placed on one's role in life, and they think about how they are perceived by others. They believe NO ONE else has EVER experienced their thoughts or emotions; they are often dramatic.

- The limbic system is being developed (which perceives rewards from risk), and so these youth often take unnecessary risks (e.g., "It can't happen to me.").

Morals/Values/Autonomy

- In middle adolescence, there is increased moral reasoning, continued growth and capacity for abstract thought, and capacity to use insight. There is an increased emphasis on personal dignity and self-esteem, and personal values and opinions become less absolute.

- Social and cultural traditions regain some of their previous importance, while there is increased questioning of social and political beliefs of adults. These youth do not have a confident grasp of their identity and faith to develop an independent perspective yet. They may hold deep spiritual values or have a strong faith without having looked at it critically.

Coaching Tips for Working with Middle Adolescents

Coaches can support adolescents to build skills that will help them manage their daily lives, especially in the areas of decision-making, goal setting and achievement, stress management, and communication skills. Use mnemonic strategies to improve learning ("every good boy does fine" is a common one for music students to remember the keys e,g,b,d,f). Assist youth in learning how to develop healthy habits, such as exercise habits, eating habits, work habits, or study habits. As their capacity for future thought increases, goal setting can include longer-term goals. Engage youth in conversations related to choices, cause and effect relationships, and future plans, providing opportunities for them to explore their point of view through conversation without judgment. With future planning exercises, it is appropriate to include multiple plans and options, self-advocacy, and even marketing themselves. Give reminders for coaching appointments and create short-term goals (e.g., daily or weekly) based on long-term goals. When possible, use texting between coaching sessions to support learning and reminders.

18–21 years old = Late Adolescence
(Transitioning from High School to Adulthood)

Late adolescence has been described as "emerging adulthood", as youth are not quite fully developed and ready for the full world yet is often being required to make independent decisions that will affect their entire lives. It is often the time when physical maturity and reproductive growth is completing. We do know now from brain research that the brain continues to develop into early adulthood (some say at least until age 21 and others say until age 25). For youth struggling with mental health issues, it can take even longer. It is the prefrontal cortex that continues to develop during this stage,

Engage youth in conversations related to choices, cause and effect relationships, and future plans, providing opportunities for them to explore their point of view through communication without judgment.

and so although these youth often look and act like adults, they still may be lacking in the cognitive skills, such as the ability to differentiate conflicting thoughts, identifying potential future consequences of current actions, determining good and bad, and suppressing impulses. As youth this age are well developed, their engagement in sexual activity increases, which puts them at a higher risk for sexually transmitted diseases and pregnancy, considering they may not be thinking of future consequences. Adult obligation can be seen as the end of independence and spontaneity.

Late Adolescence Traits

Physical

- Physical maturity and reproductive growth levels off and completes during late adolescence. Youth at this stage are usually comfortable with body image and will feel more comfortable with their sexual identity.

Social/Emotional

- Sense of identity may still be developing as they are developing a new identity related to adulthood. Peers have less influence, especially on decisions and values as these youth relate more to individuals than peer group. There is an increased concern for others.

- Sexual identity is establishing, and dating partners are based on individual preferences rather than peer pressure. It is common to delay marriage yet have serious romantic and sexual relationships.

- In late adolescence, youth relate to family as an adult. Social and cultural traditions may become important. They are more capable of intimate, complex relationships, and they have a stronger sense of identity.

- The emotions are more connected to reasoning, due to brain development, which brings more emotional stability.

Thinking/Learning/Cognitive

- Abstract thought is developed. There is an increased ability to think ideas through, delay gratification, and understand long-term goals.

- Youth in this stage are often philosophical and idealistic. They think about the meaning of life and have increased concern about the future and being future oriented.

- They may still have difficulty with complex cognitive skills, such as those listed above.

Morals/Values/Autonomy

- In late adolescence, youth are establishing their ethical and moral value system. They are often interested in moral reasoning. Faith or spiritual belief is often individualized and reflective.

- Social and cultural traditions regain importance as these older youth still carry family influences and continue to build traditions and family time together.

Coaching Tips for Working with Late Adolescents

When coaching this stage of youth, remember that all youth develop at differing rates and stages. This stage may go on through the mid-20s. The difficulty with coaching this age group often lies in the fact they are legally adults and may have expectations to fulfill the general role and responsibilities of adults yet may not quite have fully developed the general life skills needed to be successful. This stress can multiply quickly if they do not get support at the beginning. At times, support for meeting basic needs will be a priority. Support skill building which impacts their daily life includes decision-making, problem-solving, goal setting and attainment, and self-awareness and confidence. Build self-advocacy and marketing, support confidence, organizational ability and skills in communication relationships and conflict resolution. Provide opportunities for youth to explore options and practice new life or social skills and support their development of stress management skills. Hands-on experience supported by coaching can help bridge gaps of knowledge and transitional difficulties. They may need support in learning how to manage changing relationships (friends/family/parents) and at this age are already dealing with how to cope with grief and loss of a loved one. Youth at this stage are likely to know how to find information but lack the skills and/or practice of using that information (e.g., they may know how to find an answer using Google, but may not have the social skill base to contact someone to request an informational interview). It is common for youth at this age to change jobs frequently as they continually are looking to combine work, play, and personal fulfillment.

Coaching Tips for Parents of Adolescents

When coaching youth, parents are often involved and frequently are the ones who are paying for the coaching of their child. Youth coaches sometimes struggle with how to work with parents, who want to understand what is going on with their child. Youth coaches frequently involve parents in a way that can support their child's coaching goals. Below, I am offering some tips for parents themselves or for youth coaches to also support parents.

Coaching Tips for PARENTS of Early Adolescents

Youth relationships with parents begin to change at this stage, as adolescents are beginning to develop their independence.

Boys may move away from a close relationship with mothers, and girls may begin to be more emotionally distant from their fathers. Youth are just realizing that their parents are not perfect, and they will often identify their faults (and point them out to their parents). Encourage parents to set clear rules and boundaries that are age appropriate, which include school expectations and knowing where they are. As their friends become more important, don't criticize or compare teens to others (other youth or other siblings or even yourself); be understanding about needs for space and privacy (parents should know of their friends and activities, yet give them some space and privacy). Be patient of excessive time taken for grooming and their desire for increased privacy. Encourage physical activity and notice how they respond to changes in themselves and their friends. Eat meals together (role model healthy eating); talk about positive peer influences, limit screen time (experts often say 1-2 hours per day is enough) and encourage physical activity. Although this age group often wants time away from parents and family (which is normal) continue to provide safe limits and supervision and encourage family relationships with extended family and friends.

Youth coaches frequently involve parents in a way that can support their child's coaching goals.

Coaching Tips for PARENTS of Middle Adolescents

Parents need to know where the teen is and make plans with them for how they can reach you; have clear expectations and follow through with consequences. Talk with your teen about safety issues, about responsibilities, expectations and then help them plan ahead for difficult or uncomfortable situations (e.g. what would you do if your friend who drove you to the party has been drinking?). Respect their opinion (even if you disagree) and don't downplay their concerns. Encourage conflict resolution and engage them in their own behavioral consequences and guidelines. Talk about changes in behavior you notice; if you see depression, ask about suicidal thoughts (seek professional help if necessary). Show interest in your teen's activities and schoolwork; encourage volunteer work and hands on experiences. Show affection to them, while respecting their boundaries (and probably not in front of their friends if they protest). Not every disagreement is a conflict; don't take it personally.

Spend time together; eat meals together and provide teens opportunities for "controlled" risky behaviors (e.g., sports, travel, a new hobby or skill). Be patient of excessive time for grooming and be respectful of their wishes for increased privacy (they are trying to get a sense of control over their changing bodies). Encourage multiple hobbies/clubs (they are often trying out their interests, which change frequently), and provide opportunities for volunteering or community service. Help them to tap into positive role models and encourage them to learn things from them (e.g., a neighbor can teach them how to fix a car; or a cousin might have ideas for jobs; a family friend might teach them about getting along with a difficult supervisor). Provide decision making opportunities (what to buy with their own money, who will be their friend)—and why, what activities to participate in) and letting them learn from their actions.

Coaching Tips for PARENTS of Late Adolescents

Late adolescence is often a welcome stage of parenting, after the common craziness of early and middle adolescence. It is common to re-gain some of your easy relationships with your teen and actually enjoy being around him/her. Regularly ask your older teen questions about what they think and believe; listen to their answers and respect their unique ideas and opinions. Talk with your older teens about their future, their goals, priorities and dreams. Discuss independent living (job or career, education, health care, money management, shopping for groceries and cooking meals); find out where they need more skills and support their learning. Continue to spend time with your older adolescent; give them hugs and tell them you love them... they still need you!

Summary

By now, you probably have a good idea about the different ages and stages of adolescent development and how that knowledge can positively influence your work and coaching effectiveness with youth. In addition to the questions about how to coach certain age groups, another common issue that coaches have is related to how to differentiate if a potential client needs coaching or therapy. The next chapter will cover some areas for concern for coaches and provide information to help you consider when to consult a mental health or other professional.

What is your take-away from this chapter?

What are the implications for your work with youth?

CHAPTER 6

WHEN TO REFER TO A MENTAL HEALTH PROFESSIONAL

Mental health should be included in discussions about overall health and well-being. Many mental health disorders begin in childhood. The earlier the treatment and intervention, the more effective treatment can be and might prevent more severe symptoms in adulthood. Professional coaches need to know their strengths and their own limitations, especially when it comes to treating youth with underlying mental health issues. A therapist may use coaching skills in practice; a coach **may not** do therapy in the midst of a coaching relationship. This would be considered unethical and a violation of professional coaching boundaries even if you have a license to practice therapy! For coaches who have little or no training in mental health, the idea of needing to refer a client for therapy can be tricky and even scary. However, it is your professional and ethical responsibility to refer mental health issues that you cannot treat to other professionals. One of the first coaches to bring this to light is Lynne Meinke[10] one of my foundational coach trainers at Institute for Life Coach Training. It was she who wrote "Top 10 indicators of when to refer to a mental health professional" for coaches, which was posted on the ICF website. The purpose of this chapter is related to the core principles section of the Supportive Youth Coaching Model to help you understand the importance of educating yourself on early warning signs of mental illness. It is important to understand that this chapter alone will not provide enough education for you but will give you some insight into the distinctions.

One of the easiest ways for coaches to prepare is first by establishing clear and ethical guidelines in the agreement *prior* to the beginning of coaching. This way you will have the ability to pre-screen your clients to see if they are a) a good fit for coaching, and b) a good fit for you and your skills. It is possible to engage in a coaching relationship with a youth who already has a therapist; however, I would recommend appropriate permissions be signed up-front so that the therapist is aware of the coaching, and the coaching can *complement* the work in therapy.

Children's Mental Health

The first onset of most mental health disorders usually occurs in childhood or adolescence (through mid-20's), although many of these disorders are not treated until adulthood. The National Institute of Mental Health (NIMH) reported in 2005 that half of the

10   www.lifecoachtraining.com/main/profile/lynn_meinke_pcc

mental illnesses begin by age 14 and three quarters by age 24.[11] In 2013, the Center for Disease Control (CDC) published the first report of its kind to describe the vast number of US children aged 3-17 who have specific mental health disorders and described this as an important public health issue with an estimated annual cost of $247 billion.[12] In January 2019, NIMH reported from a national study that 49.5% of adolescents between the ages of 13-18 had a mental illness.[13] Professional Educator Licensing and Standards Board for Minnesota has consistently required teachers to have continuing education hours in mental health concerns in students each time they renew their teaching license. There are multiple national and state websites that list the statistic of one in five or 20% of adolescents have a diagnosable mental health disorder and that suicide is the third leading cause of death in adolescents and young adults. There are many mental health symptoms that begin in childhood and adolescence, and if untreated they may continue into adulthood.

One of the easiest ways for coaches to prepare is first by establishing clear and ethical guidelines in the agreement prior to the beginning of coaching.

Common Warning Signs

There are many locations where common warning signs of mental health issues in children and adolescents can be found, and they may vary a little, yet are very similar. This list below is published on the NIMH site[14] and is for parents, for professionals, and even for youth themselves—to help with education and early intervention.

11   www.nimh.nih.gov/news/science-news/2005/mental-illness-exacts-heavy-toll-beginning-in-youth.shtml

12   www.cdc.gov/mmwr/preview/mmwrhtml/su6202a1.htm?s_cid=su6202a1_w

13   www.nimh.nih.gov/health/statistics/mental-illness.shtml

14   www.nimh.nih.gov/health/topics/child-and-adolescent-mental-health/index.shtml

"Your child or teen might need help if he or she:

- Often feels anxious or worried

- Has frequent tantrums or is intensely irritable much of the time

- Has frequent stomachaches or headaches with no physical explanation

- Is in constant motion, can't sit quietly for any length of time

- Has trouble sleeping, including frequent nightmares

- Loses interest in things he or she used to enjoy

- Avoids spending time with friends

- Has trouble doing well in school, or grades decline

- Fears gaining weight; exercises, diets obsessively

- Has low or no energy

- Has spells of intense, inexhaustible activity

- Harms herself/himself, such as cutting or burning her/his skin

- Engages in risky, destructive behavior

- Harms self or others

- Smokes, drinks, or uses drugs

- Has thoughts of suicide

- Thinks his or her mind is controlled or out of control, hears voices"

Adolescents with mental health disorders have a high failure and dropout rate, and they often end up in juvenile detention centers, harm themselves, or harm others. The reason it is important for children and adolescents to receive care for mental health is that most mental health issues can be treated. Prevention, early intervention, and treatment of mental health issues are key to reducing additional serious problematic behavior, can lessen the duration and severity of the illness, and may reduce the likelihood of secondary disorders or more severe mental illness in adulthood. Early intervention also reduces the stress on the individual and their family.

The Client Who Never Was

I'll tell you about one of my great clients who never was. I'll call her Liza. Liza's mother contacted me about coaching her 13-year-old daughter, who had recently been struggling with school attendance and following rules at home. In my initial coaching intake with parents who call to ask me to coach their child, I ask questions about frequency, intensity, and duration of any problematic issues. I also ask what has previously been done to address the concerns. The mother stated that they had tried counseling for Liza, but that it did not work because Liza refused to talk, so the parents were thinking that maybe a life coach would be the best option. After talking and gathering more background information, I agreed to meet with the parents and Liza together to discuss life coaching and make a decision about moving forward.

In the in-person meeting with Liza and her parents, it became obvious that the parents were at their wits end in how to make Liza follow their rules, while Liza exhibited some clear markers for major depression and anxiety and was engaging in some extremely risky behaviors. As a trained therapist, I could recognize some of these issues and concerns. After meeting with Liza and her parents together and then Liza by herself, I determined that coaching would *not* be appropriate at this time. However, I did believe that Liza was in serious need of an intervention. I spoke with Liza about some of her issues while her parents were not present (part of my initial intake agreement). She readily engaged with me and admitted to suicidal ideation. I talked with her about the differences between coaching and therapy and then talked with her about how therapy could support her emotional health and get her feeling good enough to engage in a coaching relationship.

Prior to bringing back her parents, I determined with Liza how I would talk to her parents about her thoughts of suicide, and that she had agreed to try therapy again. After explaining my decision to the parents (with Liza present), they agreed to find another therapist. Since my website clearly states my qualifications and background, they asked if I would be Liza's therapist. In fact, Liza herself said she would work with me. I declined and explained my rationale. (I was not seeing private therapy clients at that time.) I then referred Liza and her parents to a few different local community clinics and gave them some tips on how to find the right therapist for Liza.

End Note:

About a year after I met with Liza and her parents, I received an email from her mother. "*Thank you again for meeting with us and talking with Liza about trying therapy again. We found her a great therapist, who she really likes, and she has been working hard in therapy on a regular basis. She was hospitalized for a brief time last year, but she is much better now. Her grades have improved, and we are enjoying having our daughter back. I'm not sure all coaches would have referred us elsewhere, but I really appreciate your integrity.*"

Aren't Mood Swings Normal?

Adolescence is already a time when mood swings are apparent and normal, compounded by hormonal changes. How in the world can coaches learn to identify what is not considered normal? Although the range of what is normal is wide, youth who develop a mental illness will often display more severe symptoms than their peers. It is important to pay attention to frequency, duration, and intensity of these symptoms. Symptoms are what we see, observe, and are reported to us that parents might be concerned about. Youth may also report these symptoms or their teachers may report them. Any time a parent or professional feels overwhelmed or concerned about a child or adolescent, it is wise to seek the support and opinions of others. Early intervention with problems helps to prevent more serious problem development. It is important to know that youth who exhibit any of the warning signs listed above do not necessarily qualify for a mental health diagnosis. This list is not exhaustive, but it can be used as a guideline to help others know when outside support could be beneficial.

If parents are uncertain where to turn for mental health help, insurance (if they have it) is a good place to start. Another option is through local community resources that provide services to youth in your client's age range. Professional life coaching for youth or adults is not covered under any health insurance plan at this time. Health coaching sometimes is covered and is a different type of coaching. However, the costs of mental health services are usually covered by insurance. If the family does not have insurance, many communities have non-profit organizations that provide either pro-bono or sliding-fee therapy services.

> **Youth who develop a mental illness will often display more severe symptoms than their peers.**

It is interesting to note that even in adults, there are many untreated and undiagnosed mental health issues. There is some evidence and concern that adults with mental health issues choose coaching over therapy, as coaching appears to some as a more acceptable form of support. What this means, though, is that some coaches engage in a professional coaching relationship with clients who would be best served by a mental health professional. Yet, unless coaches are aware of mental health signs and symptoms, he/she may not refer the client and the coaching may end unsuccessfully.

Summary

As a professional life coach, you do not have the responsibility to be trained in treating mental health issues. It is your ethical responsibility, however, to recognize when coaching may not be appropriate or the best option for the client or when to realize that a mental health issue may be getting in the way of successful coaching and refer them to more appropriate resources. Being aware of when to refer a coaching client (or potential client) falls into ethical considerations for coaches and will be discussed further in the next chapter.

What is your take-away from this chapter?

What are the implications for your work with youth?

CHAPTER 7

ETHICAL CONSIDERATIONS WHEN COACHING MINOR YOUTH

The ethical issues discussed in this chapter are particular to coaching youth under the age of 18 (minor youth). The concept of professional life coaching is based on principles of adult learning and working with adults, so those coaching youth are often left trying to figure out where to find guidance. This chapter is related to the core principles section of the Supportive Youth Coaching Model discussed in Chapter 4. It is imperative for coaches to follow a code of ethics and even better if that code is supported and sponsored by a professional association. The intent behind a code of ethics is to provide an ethical framework and values upon which a practice is based. Ethical issues in coaching can arise in many areas and coaches need to have the ability to make appropriate ethical decisions. This is especially true when coaching minor youth, due to the multitude of laws and expectations related to the protection of minor youth. It is my belief and experience that the majority (but not all) of mistakes made in youth coaching fall under the realm of ethics.

Most coach training organizations around the world support coaches following a code of ethics. I also strongly encourage all coaches to be clear about the ethical codes to which they adhere, and to share this information with their clients. It is perfectly acceptable for a coach to follow more than one code of ethics. For example, as a licensed clinical social worker, I follow the Minnesota Board of Social Work's Ethical Standards of Practice, which is based on Minnesota laws. I also am a member of the National Association of Social Workers (NASW) and follow the NASW Code of Ethics. And as a certified professional coach (PPC) through the ICF, I follow their code of ethics. The code governing a clinical licensure, even when practicing as a coach, always supersedes the coaching code of ethics. The ICF is only one of many coaching organizations for professional coaches, and they have done much work in developing their code of ethics. Since it is the one with which I am most familiar, I will be using the ICF code of ethics as a basis for discussion here, knowing that other coaches may have ethics codes from other professional organizations. Most codes of ethics include areas of professional conduct, conflicts of interest, confidentiality and

It is my belief and experience that the majority (but not all) of mistakes made in youth coaching fall under the realm of ethics.

privacy as well as continuing education and development. These codes are there to help inform and guide us while also providing protection for our clients.

Scenario

Prior to our discussion on some of the nuances in coaching minor youth, I'd like you to consider the following scenario:

Jill is a new life coach. She has completed an approved number of coaching hours, has completed her ICF certification requirements, and is just waiting to take the final oral exam. Jill has a master's degree and has been working as a therapist for 15 years. She decided life coaching would complement her current skills and provide her with a new revenue stream of clients. She receives a call from a parent of a 16-year-old girl named Tania, who wants to hire Jill to coach her daughter. Tania's mother received Jill's name from another parent in her daughter's school. Tania is a smart student, she explained, but began the school year with difficulty, and her grades have dropped to Cs and Ds. The mother believes it has to do with her recent divorce, her daughter feeling like she doesn't fit in, and low self-esteem. Based on the initial conversation, Jill informs the mother that Tania needs support not only with academics, but with her mood changes, as she appears to be struggling with depression. Jill explained that aside from being a certified life coach, she has many years of experience as a therapist working with depressed girls like Tania.

Jill assures the mother she can help Tania with her depression, suggesting she may be dealing with effects from the divorce two years ago and the adjustment to the new normal of life. She also let the mother know life coaching has a proven track record with academic issues and assures her coaching will result in her daughter's grades returning to As. Jill gets some more background information, describes how coaching works and tells the mother her coaching fee. The mother believes this will be perfect for Tania and had already informed Tania she is going to sign her up for life coaching.

They agree coaching will begin after school the following week. Jill said she knows the school principal and would be able to arrange for an empty classroom where they can meet. They agree the coaching will take place once a week at school for a total of 10 sessions. Jill informs the mother that by meeting at school, she can have easy access to Tania's teachers to get information about how Tania is doing in school and share Tania's coaching goals with the school staff. Jill accepts payment via credit card over the phone and schedules the first coaching appointment with Tania for the following week. Jill lets the mother know she will follow up each coaching session with a detailed email of everything talked about in coaching so she can support her daughter's coaching process. The mother assures Jill she will explain everything to Tania prior to their first coaching session. Tania's mother is not able to be at the first coaching appointment, but Jill assures mom, she is welcome to sit in on any of the coaching sessions, as long as she agrees not to interrupt or say anything during the session.

At the first coaching session, Jill talks with Tania about coaching, her background and the goals Tania will be working on (grades and mood). Tania seems engaged and set some initial goals around school grades. Towards the end of the first session, Tania shares some feelings with Jill related to her feeling depressed but doesn't want her mom to know. Jill then explains to Tania that the coaching agreement with her mother includes sharing information discussed in each session with both her mother and the school staff so they can all support Tania with her goals. Tania becomes angry and walks out of the session stating she doesn't want to meet again. Jill later shares with Tania's mother details of the session and how it ended with Tania walking out. They agree Jill should give Tania some time and try again next week. Tania later told her mother she would not meet with Jill again, but the mother tells Jill to keep trying in case her daughter changes her mind. For the next nine weeks (to the end of the pre-paid coaching agreement), Jill goes to the school to meet with Tania, who continues to refuse to meet with her.

ICF Code of Ethics and Coach Jill

What went wrong? Could you see the eight red flags I've included in this scenario? As you read the rest of the chapter, keep this scenario in mind. Regardless of whether you are a coach or belong to a coaching association, this discussion will be relevant to ethical issues in working with youth.

Discussion

At times, those of us who coach youth are unequivocally excited and motivated about how great coaching works with teens and young adults. This is good. However, when our enthusiasm and confidence lead to promises or assurances that our clients will benefit from coaching, this behavior leaks into the area of unethical behavior. It would have been better for Jill to talk with the mother and Tania about the benefits of and past successes of coaching, but not to assure change will happen. There is a research study that supports the notion that youth who have received coaching have a reduction in depression; there is no evidence to support the claim that coaching is an effective intervention for depression.

In the scenario, Jill told the mother that she was a certified life coach through the ICF, when in fact, she hadn't quite completed the process and was not yet certified. This statement was an ethical violation related to being honest and accurate about credentials, qualifications, etc., as well as that of the coaching profession. Ethical behavior includes how we talk about our services, our profession, and ourselves in an accurate manner. Of course, we need to believe in our services and have confidence, or we would make poor business owners. In my coaching agreements, I offer no guarantees. I do, however, offer money-back for dissatisfied clients. Thus far, I've yet to have a client request money back.

When coaching minor youth, the youth is still the client (not the parent). The conversation and coaching agreement above took place between Jill and Tania's mother. Tania is the client and her mother would be considered a sponsor or the person paying for the coaching. It is unethical to contract with a sponsor (e.g., parent who is paying for the coaching) without involving the client. The child or teen also needs to be included in the conversation about confidentiality and the parameters around it (and agree to it). Coaching is voluntary and attempting to force a youth into coaching will usually result in a failed coaching experience.

In the above example, sharing what is discussed in Tania's coaching session with her mother without Tania's knowledge or consent would be unethical. Anything shared with the parent needs to be with permission and agreement from the client. Coaching ethical guidelines are similar to those of other professions (healthcare, mental health) in that the client has the right to confidentiality from the sponsor. Regardless of whether a parent is paying for the service, the coach cannot ethically share information from the coaching sessions with a minor client without clear permission, up-front conversations, and agreements from that minor child. Depending on the age of the youth, developmental issues, relationship with the parent, etc., these decisions about sharing information need to be discussed prior to the start of coaching as well as on an on-going basis.

Jill also would not be able to show up at the school and use a school classroom (or even talk to the school about using a classroom to meet with this student) without written permission from the mother to talk to the school about Tania. This is often called a "Release of Information". And then, even if the parent gives written permission, Tania (as the coaching client) would also need to give her permission.

I strongly advocate coaches find a way to include the parent or guardian in ways that will support the client's success. Parental involvement and support are often crucial to the success of youth achieving their goals. Minor children who are living at home are often unable to even set or achieve goals without their parent's knowledge and support. The goal may require youth to have permission or transportation (e.g., go to the library, stay after school, leave home to exercise, study, etc.). The key here is **creating a plan with the client** as to what they are comfortable sharing, where they are comfortable meeting as well as the best way to share this information.

Unfortunately, some youth coaches make the mistake of allowing the parent to make decisions about details of the coaching rather than the youth. Many of these situations could be avoided by the coach doing a better job of including **the youth** at the beginning of the information sharing and decision-making

> Minor children who are living at home are often unable to even set or achieve goals without their parent's knowledge and support.

prior to the start of coaching. However, once a parent has paid and the youth has started, some coaches have a difficult time allowing youth to stop (or change) the process, and instead struggle with non-engagement and multiple no-shows for appointments. In the above example, Tania was clearly upset with Jill, the coach, and did not want to meet with her again. Jill was not respecting Tania's right to terminate the coaching agreement. I probably would have tried at least once to talk again with Tania and see if it was possible to re-establish a coaching agreement with her; however, to continue to ignore the fact that Tania had no interest in meeting with her would be considered a breach of ethics. Coaching is voluntary. At no time should a required relationship be considered coaching.

It sounds confusing, but it really is not. Most issues related to confidentiality can be easily resolved prior to the start of coaching with a clear coaching agreement that is explained in detail to both the parent and the minor client.

Coaching agreements are not required to be in writing; however, this would be the clearest and cleanest way to do business as a professional coach. It is one way to put protections in place for the client as well as the coach. Yet, many coaches do not have a written or signed agreement. In my research, I found that the majority of youth coaches do (most likely as youth workers they are more familiar with ethical issues related to working with minor youth).

Additional Thoughts on Ethics and Minor Youth

There is a large population of underserved youth who are not living at home but may be receiving services through youth-serving organizations that have cleared the legalities of working with youth such as those who are experiencing homelessness, sex-trafficking, foster care or group home living. And the majority of these youth are disproportionately youth of color and/or LGBTQ+ youth who could really benefit from life coaching. In Minnesota, we have The Homeless Youth Act which allows organizations to provide services and support to homeless or at risk of homelessness youth aged 24 or younger to provide their own consent for services.[15] It would be opportune for these agencies as well are schools to hire professional life coaches to work with these youth.

I'd like to mention another ethical issue for organizations that hire coaches to work with youth. Coaches who hire other coaches to work with minor clients need to also be trained in the above ethics. The caveat of this particular part of the code is that in many locations/states, anyone who works directly with minor youth in a professional capacity is either required or strongly suggested to have a background check through the Bureau of Criminal Apprehensions prior to working directly with minor youth. This is for the protection of the children. If you are a coach who employs other coaches to work with minor clients, those employees should pass a background check prior to working with minor youth. I also recommend checking with the state statutes as the laws differ from state to state.

Referring Elsewhere

In the last chapter, we talked about when to refer to a mental health professional. This is a challenge for working with both teen and adult clients. The caveat here is in understanding mental health issues in youth, which are often manifested differently than in adults. For example, in some children and youth, depression will manifest as an anger problem rather than sadness. The previous chapter discusses the importance of coaches being able to refer clients or potential clients elsewhere when appropriate.

15   www.mn.gov/dhs/assets/2017-02-homeless-youth-act-report_tcm1053-280441.pdf

It is also important that a coach be able (and willing) to refer clients or potential clients elsewhere, where they may be more appropriately served. The coach who is not familiar with or qualified to provide appropriate services to meet a client's needs should refer elsewhere. Reasons for referral could include the coach not being comfortable with a certain culture, unable or unwilling to provide an interpreter for language needs, and a coach who is not comfortable or familiar with adolescent development.

This part of the ethical code is not different for adult clients. The difference lies in the fact that many professionally trained coaches believe they are automatically qualified to coach children because of their life experience (they once went through adolescence). Some coaches are so far removed from working with teenagers they have unrealistic standards for coaching this age group. Examples of this concern come from comments from coaches reporting struggles with their teen clients:

- *"I'm not so sure coaching works with teens; any time I've had a teen client, they end up forgetting appointments and not working on the goals we set between sessions."*

- *"I don't really like working with teenagers, and my focus is corporate coaching... but when my biggest client asked me to coach their teenager as a favor, I didn't want to say no."*

- *"The student I was coaching just told me what I wanted to hear, and I had no idea they were actually failing their classes; I guess coaching doesn't work for this age group."*

These three comments came from coaches who, I believe, should refer these teen clients to another coach who understands and enjoys working with teens. Or they could benefit from hiring a mentor coach when working with teens. A part of ethical coaching includes knowing our own strengths and weaknesses as well as being willing to say no to potential income (clients) and referring the client to another coach, who could better serve the client.

Summary

Coaches must follow a code of ethics to both inform and guide us as coaches, as well as to protect our clients. Working with minor youth (younger than age 18) has additional ethical considerations. Now that we have a clear understanding of some of the ethical issues related to coaching youth let's take a look at the skill set needed by coaches working with youth. We will use as a base of this discussion, the ICF core competencies in which they assess the skill level for various competencies of coaches for their licensure.

What is your take-away from this chapter?

What are the implications for your work with youth?

CHAPTER 8

CORE COMPETENCIES FOR COACHING YOUTH

Core Competencies

Directly related to the discussion on ethical considerations, a discussion on skills and competencies for youth coaches is needed. This chapter is also related to the core principles of the Supportive Youth Coaching Model covered in Chapter 3. As I described in Chapter 2, the ICF has created 11 Core Competencies that coaches are required to master in order to become certified. Each of the three levels of certification requires a deepening of the skills in each competency. These competencies are grouped into four categories that are illustrated in the table below. This chapter is organized by these four categories and will cover some of the nuances related to coaching minor youth. Although what I'll be talking about in this chapter is based on U.S. knowledge of ethics, laws, and the legal system, it is also applicable for youth coaches worldwide.

Table 1. *ICF Core Competencies, Grouped*[16]

A. Setting the Foundation
    1. Meeting ethical guidelines and professional standards
    2. Establishing the coaching agreement

B. Co-creating the relationship
    1. Establishing trust and intimacy with the client
    2. Coaching presence

C. Communicating effectively
    1. Active listening
    2. Powerful questioning
    3. Direct communication

D. Facilitating learning and results
    1. Creating awareness
    2. Designing actions
    3. Planning and goal setting
    4. Managing progress and accountability

Setting the Foundation

This first skill category, setting the foundation, involves coaches meeting ethical and professional standards and establishing the coaching agreement. These two skill areas have the most impact on youth coaches, as it provides the base of the coaching experience.

16 www.coachfederation.org/core-competencies

You can see how this foundation overlaps with the previous chapter on ethics. Ethical issues are often confusing and interrelated. It also requires the most front work by youth coaches to ready themselves for how they will handle these issues differently than they do when coaching adults. This, of all the four sections, seems to have the most implications for youth coaches.

When meeting with a potential client about coaching, it is important for them to really understand what you are offering, the logistics and guidelines of the coaching relationship, who is responsible for what, and if there is an effective match between your coaching and the needs of the potential client. For these things to happen, an in-depth conversation needs to take place. Meeting ethical guidelines and establishing the coaching agreement often feels like a lot of extra work when working with minor youth. However, doing the work prior to the start of coaching will save you time, headaches and have a positive impact on your coaching relationship in the long run. Below, I've illustrated some distinctions for minor youth that you'll want to include as a part of the intake discussion.

> **Ethical issues are often confusing and interrelated.**

- The coach should have the conversation with both the parent and child/client. As far as the logistics of coaching (how/when/where/frequency, etc.), there are some specifics to consider related to minor youth. For details, please refer to Chapter 3 under "Core Principles" in the Supportive Youth Coaching Model.

- The language used should be at the client's level of understanding both intellectually as well as developmentally (refer to Chapter 5 for information on adolescent development).

- Coaches should clearly explain the differences between coaching and therapy, and this is an excellent time to discuss how coaching is not for everyone and the possibility of referral elsewhere if deemed appropriate. By having this conversation initially, it will open the doors for further conversation with parent and child about mental health issues, if needed. (Refer to Chapter 6 for more information on mental health issues.)

- Another aspect of meeting ethical guidelines and professional standards is that you have a conversation with minor client and parent about *confidentiality*—what you will and won't share, with whom, and how that decision is made. More information on this is in the previous chapter on ethics as well as in the next few pages on potential obligations.

- The minor youth needs to be included and have control of what and how to share information with their parent (within the parameters of confidentiality). If a coach is keen on developmental issues and family relationships, they will also continue to check in with the client on issues of confidentiality throughout the coaching process. As trust is developed between the coach and client, the client's answers and willingness to share information may vary.

What about the Parent?

In my research with youth coaches around the world, those who had prior training related to adolescent development were much clearer about the ethics of confidentiality than those coaches who had little to no training on adolescent development. For youth coaches, one of the more confusing aspects is when and how to include a parent. Those coaches I surveyed who did include parents did so in varying (and conflicting) degrees, outlined by some of the comments below:

- *"I'll never include any parents while coaching youth. When (the) coach shows this trust, youth can hold it easily."*

- *"I always include the parent(s) in the coaching when the client is financially reliant on the parent(s) because the client's performance/work is always tied in with the family system."*

- *"All work is done with parents present."*

Some coaches limit parental involvement based on what the youth want and agree to:

- *"Parents are always aware of the coaching their child is receiving. The amount that they are involved depends on the agreements built between me, the young adult, and the parent."*

- *"Parents are only involved if the youth wants them to be there. If the youth is living at home, I think it is important that the parents have an awareness of the process and coaching but never share information about the sessions."*

This part of the conversation should happen prior to the start of coaching (when the youth doesn't fall under the umbrella of "homeless youth" described above). This is so both youth and parent have a clear understanding of the coaching relationship and boundaries. I'm not at all suggesting we exclude parents when coaching their minor children. In fact, in most situations, parents and guardians are a key to the success of the coaching relationship and goal accomplishment when youth are living at home. There are many ways in which parents can support their youth to succeed in coaching; however, the youth must have the upper hand in how and what is shared with their parent.

Another caveat to this competency is related to having a formal coaching agreement signed by the client (youth) and sponsor (parent). In my research, I found the majority of youth coaches used a formal written agreement. However, for those who had a formal agreement, only half of them had the parents of minor youth sign the agreement; fewer than that asked the minor youth to also sign. A formal written agreement is not required for coaching. However, it is recommended especially as it helps to clarify the coaching relationship and responsibilities. This includes potential obligations of youth coaches that are not clearly discussed in the core competencies.

Potential Obligations

Potential obligations of youth coaches who work with minor clients could include the following, depending on what state and country in which you live. In my research with youth coaches, those experienced in youth work (from the U.S. and internationally) usually covered these issues with parents and minor youth. It was coaches who were not trained youth workers who had difficulty with these potential obligations and did not consider them appropriate or of any concern for them as a coach of minor youth. It is my recommendation each coach research their own state and country and include this relevant information into their intake with minor clients and parents:

The youth must have the upper hand in how and what is shared with their parent.

- **Criminal Background Checks:** The majority of youth coaches surveyed in my research have had criminal background checks completed prior to working with youth. However, of those surveyed who have hired other coaches to work with youth, half of them did and half did *not* have criminal background checks completed on these employees. Although more common in the U.S., coaches from other countries also have had criminal background checks completed prior to working with youth. If you hire others to work for you and work with minor youth, then you should have criminal background checks completed on your employees.

- **Duty to Warn:** Although this is an American term, breaking confidentiality to alert others to potential harm is common internationally. The laws of the U.S. vary by state; it requires those involved in direct contact with minors to have a duty to warn or take precautions to protect threat of violence when the potential victim is clearly stated. In many states, a professional not following through on this can be held liable. Here is a link to the Minnesota statute.[17] Of the 50 states, 45 have specific laws outlined related to duty to protect or warn, although what varies is whether it is mandatory or permissive. It is your responsibility as a coach to find out what your state requires and to follow that mandate. The following link outlines and updates each of the 50 states and their requirements.[18]

- **Mandatory Reporting:** This law is created for the protection of minor youth. It allows the professional to break confidentiality and report suspected child abuse. Again, this law varies from state to state as well as between countries. However, it is a common law and one youth coaches need to be versed in and know how to handle. Some coaches believe they are not required to report since they are not providing therapy. However, mandatory reporting is subject to the definitions of each state and country. In Minnesota, the persons required to report include

17   www.revisor.mn.gov/statutes/?id=148.975
18   www.ncsl.org/research/health/mental-health-professionals-duty-to-warn.aspx

professionals engaged in healing arts, social services, and education (among others) and coaching could fall under various areas. The Minnesota statute is here.[19] Coaches have been extremely confused about whether or not they are required to report. As with duty to warn, it is the ethical responsibility of the coach to know their own state's laws and adhere to them. Each of the 50 states has laws related to mandatory reporting.[20]

- **Parental Consent:** In some situations, a minor may give consent to be treated for certain health issues; however, most states require parent or guardian's consent prior to working with a minor youth in a professional capacity. There are exceptions of course (e.g., drop-in centers, homeless and runaway youth programs); however, when youth are living at home and under the age of 18, I suggest parental consent be a requirement for youth coaches. When I was coaching in a high school, the school did take care of the parental consent for me, yet it was my responsibility to be sure it was completed prior to the start of coaching.

In my coaching intake, I cover all these areas with the minor youth and the parent and explain the reasons why it is important (for the protection of the youth). I like to be clear about explaining the parameters of confidentiality, and I take my work with them seriously. Many teens know all about these four issues and will not be surprised; but for some youth, this might be new information.

In the scenario in Chapter 7, if Tania is an appropriate coaching client for Jill, then as a part of her discussion with Tania and her mother (together), Jill could talk about these logistical areas and come to some agreement. For example, will Tania need a ride to and

19   www.ncsl.org/research/health/mental-health-professionals-duty-to-warn.aspx

20   www.childwelfare.gov/responding/mandated.cfm

from coaching? Is the coaching in person or on the phone? If they want to coach at the school, is that OK with Tania? Tania's mother will need to sign a release of information form for Jill to talk to the school and see if the school is open for them to meet after school on the school grounds. The school should require a background check on Jill prior to allowing her to meet in the school. Can Tania call, text or email Jill in-between sessions? Will Jill give a reminder to Tania and/or her mother about coaching appointments? Will Jill focus on grades for Tania during the coaching sessions, even if Tania is not interested in improving her grades? How and what information about coaching will be shared with Tania's mom? What if Tania doesn't want her mom to know what she's talking about? How will Jill handle confidentiality? These are just a few examples of possible conversations related to this competency.

The last part of setting the foundation is for the coach to determine if this is the right client for the coach, if the coach is appropriate for the client, and if the client is ready for coaching. If all three of these are not in alignment, then it is the coach's responsibility to refer the client elsewhere and talk about what it might look like when the client is ready. The reason this competency is a little different when coaching minor children is because most often it is the parent hiring the coach for their child. Usually the parent is sold on coaching before they even make the first contact. It is the youth (the client) who needs to be ready and willing to engage in coaching.

Co-creating the Relationship

The art of co-creating the coaching relationship includes the ability to establish a strong relationship while remaining present throughout the coaching process. For youth coaching, the key aspects here are related to setting and maintaining appropriate boundaries and managing strong emotions. Youth coaches need to create and maintain clear boundaries while coaching youth. Although this is also key for coaching adults, the difference lies in that youth are not fully developed and may rely on and be more easily influenced or be taken advantage of due to their developmental stage. When coaching minor youth, the life coach will always have the "power" in the relationship. It is the responsibility of the coach to clarify and maintain healthy boundaries. Delineation of roles and responsibilities is essential when coaching youth.

Another part of maintaining a coaching presence includes demonstrating confidence in working with strong emotions. After reading Chapter 6 on developmental issues, you'll remember a part of youth is dealing with strong emotions, which are often confusing and surprising. Adults who work with youth need to be confident working with strong emotions, can self-manage and not be overpowered or enmeshed by a client's emotions. Depending on their level of development and age, teens often have unreliable and uncontrolled emotional reactions due to the hormonal changes they are experiencing. The most important aspect of this competency is the ability to not take it personally. Youth coaches need to have a thick skin and be willing and able to allow youth to explore the many emotional responses they may have, without judgment or negative reaction.

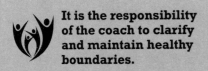

It is the responsibility of the coach to clarify and maintain healthy boundaries.

Communicating Effectively

These aspects of communication are a key to the success of coaching, and there is little difference in work with adults and with youth. One consideration here for coaching minor youth is having the ability to understand the development of the youth and communicate at their level of understanding. The coach may need to adjust and adapt his or her own language and use analogies and metaphors the youth can understand. A simple example is how coaches talk about goals. Not all kids know what a goal is or what it means to set one. A part of your communication will be to ensure you know what they are talking about (ask them when you don't understand their language), and they know what you are talking about. (You may need to explain some concepts you think are simple to understand.)

Facilitating Learning and Results

This last section of the core competencies is all about the coach helping the client have a positive learning and successful results from the coaching process. For minor youth, the goal setting and accountability seems to be one the biggest challenges for youth coaches (and parents). A key to this is the set up (creating awareness and designing actions). I think it's really hard for us NOT to tell kids what they should do and how they should do it. After all, we're adults. We've been around, and we really do know what is best. The problem is, this is not coaching. Some youth coaches struggle with this part of the core competencies because they are quick to make suggestions and might (purposefully or inadvertently) try to get the client to agree to what they want them to work on. Because kids are impressionable, they will often agree when they know it is what we want them to do, even if they really don't want to do it! Which then leads to goals that are not accomplished and sometimes a failed coaching relationship. It might be easy to blame the youth and say that they weren't ready for coaching. But the truth might be that the coach was not skilled enough in relationship building, creating awareness and designing actions. The beauty of coaching is connecting the client to their own goals and dreams and the motivation to really *want* to achieve a goal they set.

Developmentally, adolescence is a time to learn and practice skills, which will eventually support their successful transition into adulthood. Setting and achieving goals is not only central to life coaching, but it is the foundation of self-regulation. Goal setting is related to the core methods part of the Supportive Youth Coaching Model in Chapter 4. Youth coaches need to understand goal setting and that achievement with youth may be different than with adults due to the youth's development. So, it is important for coaches to understand youth may need to frequently re-adjust and adapt their goals. Also, depending on age and development, the brain is not fully developed.

The prefrontal cortex area of our brains is responsible for integrating logic with emotions, making judgments and decisions, and controls impulses. This is not the only reason, but one example of why it is important for youth coaches to understand youth development. If you look at the chapter on adolescent development, you will see examples where, depending on their developmental stage, youth may have difficulty setting goals that are more than a week in advance. Youth may benefit from more frequent check-ins and reminders than adults.

They may need more assistance in breaking down a goal into smaller, more manageable steps to avoid being overwhelmed. If you review the developmental stages, you'll see how asking a 12-year-old to set a goal related to their future should be shorter term and more immediate than when setting goals with a 17-year-old.

Youth coaches need to understand goal setting and that achievement with youth may be different than with adults due to the youth's development.

Summary

Whether or not you are a part of the ICF, the skills listed above are key skills for youth coaches to incorporate for the best experience for their youth coaching clients. The full list of the ICF Core Competencies can be found on the ICF website.[21] In this next chapter, we'll be discussing emotional intelligence and youth.

21   www.coachfederation.org/core-competencies

What is your take-away from this chapter?

What are the implications for your work with youth?

LET'S START
THE JOURNEY

CHAPTER 9

EMOTIONAL INTELLIGENCE IN YOUTH

This chapter focuses on emotional intelligence, how it fits with youth coaching, and why it is important for youth. Emotional intelligence (EI) is related to the core methods part of the Supportive Youth Coaching Model from Chapter 4. It is one of the important skill building areas for youth development.

There is plenty out there on the importance of emotional intelligence for both adults and youth. EI has become popular with the corporate and business world, who are utilizing EI assessments and coaching for managers and leaders as they see a huge financial benefit to the business. The Collaborative for Academic, Social, and Emotional Learning (CASEL) has been promoting social and emotional learning (SEL) for youth for years. The Illinois Department of Education has a comprehensive curriculum for SEL with specific standards set for each grade from kindergarten through the 12th grade. The research on Positive Youth Development indicates the importance of assisting youth to build social and emotional development. Research on the Multi-Health System Inc. Emotional Quotient-Inventory 2.0® (EQ-i 2.0®) assessment demonstrates how those with higher emotional intelligence tend to have more success academically, socially, and professionally. This chapter is about what EI is, and how emotional intelligence not only supports youth workers in their ability to more positively impact the lives of youth, but also how and why it is key for youth development. The majority of information presented in this chapter is summarized or reprinted with permission from Multi-Health Systems (MHS)[22] as I am certified in the EQ-i 2.0 assessments. The section under "application to children" has been generously supplied by Dr. Korrel Kanoy of Developmental Associates. Dr. Kanoy is also a co-author of a book I highly recommend[23] that is an excellent resource for understanding how important emotional intelligence is for youth.

EI: What Is It?

Emotional intelligence is a concept that describes factors that set successful leaders ahead of others. MHS describes EI as "a set of emotional and social skills that influence the way we perceive and express ourselves, develop and maintain social relationships, cope with challenges, and use emotional information in an effective and meaningful way (MHS, 2011)." CASEL defines social and emotional

---

22   www.mhs.com

23   *The Student EQ Edge: Emotional Intelligence and your Academic and Personal Success* by Stein, Book and Kanoy (2013)

learning as "the process through which children and adults acquire and effectively apply the knowledge, attitudes, and skills they need to understand and manage emotions, set and accomplish positive goals, feel and show empathy for others, establish and maintain positive relationships, and make responsible decisions."[24] Daniel Goleman talks about the importance of SEL for children, "...helping children improve their self-awareness and confidence, manage their disturbing emotions and impulses, and increase their empathy pays off not just in improved behavior but in measurable academic achievement."[25]

We start developing our EI as infants and continue to learn as we age. EI is a set of skills that we can develop and improve upon at any age. When youth learn and have the opportunity to practice EI skills, their positive behaviors are increased, and negative behaviors decreased. Studies on middle, high school, and college youth showed no difference between gender, ethnic, or racial origin and their scores on the EQ-i 2.0 assessments. This assessment cuts across the gender gap, can be applied throughout a range of multicultural settings, as there appears to be no *emotional* advantages or disadvantages of being a man or a woman from any race or culture. The 15 skills described in this chapter will help you to understand how EI skills impact our daily lives, and why it is essential to support youth learning and practicing EI skills.

Adults who work with youth cannot adequately support youth learning these crucial skills, without being able to appropriately role model and display emotional intelligence. Healthy, successful adults are most able to support the success of today's youth. Emotional

---

24 www.casel.org/social-and-emotional-learning/core-competencies

25 www.danielgoleman.info/topics/emotional-intelligence

intelligence is not a trend or a fad. Good relationships and coping strategies have been and are a key to our success in every area of life. EI can be learned, practiced, and improved upon at home, at school, and individually. Individuals with higher EI generally have more success at home, work, in school, and in their relationships with others. Youth who have support in improving their EI have better academic success, lower behavioral problems, and live healthier lives.

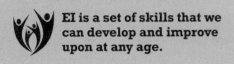

EI is a set of skills that we can develop and improve upon at any age.

A Little Bit about the Brain

As adults who work with youth, we generally want to influence the behavior of youth. To effectively influence others' behavior, you must first effectively manage your own. Many attempts to change behavior of youth fail because we focus on the behavior itself. Our behavior and that of others does not just happen in a vacuum. The building blocks of behavior are the ways that people think about that situation AND how they feel (emotions). Attempts to change that behavior without changing the underlying thoughts and feelings might result in short-term change... But change that is not aligned with underlying thoughts and feelings will be short-lived. Have you ever tried to start a new habit or drop a bad habit of yours? It could be anything from trying to quit smoking, to losing weight, to going to the gym, or even keeping your home picked up. Are you like me, in that this new habit works for a while, but then you slip back into the old habit? It is human nature that when people are not focused on their new behavior, their old habits (based on their feelings and thoughts) will re-emerge. EI focuses on helping us learn about our thinking and how it influences our emotions and therefore our behavior.

Our thoughts influence our emotions, and sometimes a part of our brain (the amygdala) jumps to respond to an event, bypassing our thought process. Because the brains of youth are not fully developed, they generally have more difficulty with decision-making, problem-solving, and impulsivity than adults. Youth don't have the life experience adults do to practice building effective behaviors that build neuronal pathways to help make these behaviors more automatic.

If events controlled our emotions, we would all be helpless victims. Learning about brain development and realizing that we can change our feelings by changing our thinking about an event, helps to control our emotions. The fact that interpretations control our emotional response means that we can manage our emotions, AND we can teach kids to do the same! Much of what we fear, what makes us mad, what makes us feel safe is established in childhood when our logic is underdeveloped. As we mature, our logic skills develop. However, our emotional responses are not automatically updated, *unless we work on it.* Building EI skills can allow us to rewire our emotional patterns to create some new default responses. Adolescence is the prime time for the development of emotional and social competencies as well as re-wiring emotional patterns while they are less developed.

Learning emotional intelligence skills begins in early childhood and continues throughout our lives. Although IQ is important, it is EI that helps us be successful by learning to think about how we feel and use these thoughts and emotions to help us solve problems and interact

> **Adolescence is the prime time for development of emotional and social competencies as well as re-wiring emotional patterns while they are less developed.**

with others. Key sought-after behaviors in the workplace include problem-solving, decision-making and communicating with others effectively both inside and outside of the organization. These are EI skills in action.

EQ-i Model by Multi-Health Systems

EI has been around since about 1983 starting with Reuven Bar-On, and more recently in 1995 Daniel Goleman helped us realize that these so-called soft skills are crucial in not only our everyday lives, but in our business and school success. The following information is taken from the EQ-i 2.0 assessment by MHS (©Multi-Health Systems, Inc.).

The EQ-i 2.0 is a self-assessment with 133 questions. It assesses 15 different skills, categories into the following 5 areas: 1. Self-perception, 2. Self-expression, 3. Interpersonal, 4. Decision-making, and 5. Stress management. The EQ-i 2.0 Work Place report is 21 pages and details each of the five areas as well as each individual skill; then it provides you with specific concrete suggestions for balancing your own EI. MHS designed many different types of reports based on the EQ-i 2.0 model. These reports are: EQ-i 2.0 Workplace (for any adult or older youth), EQ-i 2.0 Leadership Report, EQ-i 2.0 Group Report, EQ-I 2.0 360 Report, EQ-I 2.0 Group Report, and EQ-i 2.0 Higher Ed. Report. It is the Higher Ed Report that is most helpful for older youth, and it was created to support the health, success, and well-being of college students. It can also be used for older youth in high school preparing for adulthood, whether that be higher education or in developing necessary skills to be successful at work. Next, I'll review the 15 skills included in the EQ-i 2.0 assessments by MHS.

EQ-i 2.0 subscales of Emotional Intelligence
© 2011 MHS, Inc. Reprinted with permission.
Self-Regard: The ability to respect and accept yourself as basically good and to like who you are "warts and all."
Emotional Self-Awareness: The ability to recognize your feelings and to know why you are feeling a certain way.
Assertiveness: The ability to express feelings, beliefs, and thoughts and to defend your rights without threatening others.
Self-Actualization: The ability to realize your potential capacities through involvement in pursuits that have meaning for you.
Independence: The ability to be self-reliant in your thinking and actions; to be free of emotional dependency.
Empathy: The ability to be aware of, to understand, and to care about the feelings of others; to be able to read other people.
Social Responsibility: The ability to be a cooperative, contributing, and constructive member of your social groups.
Interpersonal Relationship: The ability to create and maintain mutually satisfying relationships that are characterized by intimacy and affection.
Problem-Solving: The ability to methodically confront, identify and define problems as well as to generate and implement potentially effective solutions.

Reality Testing: The ability to see things as they are, rather than as we wish or fear them to be; to keep feelings from overwhelming our perception of objective facts.

Flexibility: The ability to adjust our emotions, thoughts, and behavior to changing situations.

Stress Tolerance: The ability to handle bad events and stressful situations without "falling apart"; to manage through active and positive coping techniques.

Impulse Control: The ability to resist or delay an impulse or temptation to act; to be able to tolerate frustration without loss of control.

I. Self-Perception

Self-perception is the first category and is made up of the skills self-regard, self-actualization and emotional self-awareness. Self-perception can be described as the "inner-self". It is designed to assess feelings of inner strength and confidence, persistence in the pursuit of personally relevant and meaningful goals while understanding what, when, why, and how different emotions impact thoughts and actions. *"Success in this area means you are aware of your feelings, feel confident, and have direction and meaning in pursuing your goals."* (©MHS, 2011)

II. Self-Expression

The second of the five categories is called "self-expression". It is made up of emotional expression, assertiveness, and independence. Self-expression is an extension of the self-perception scale. It addresses the outward expression or the action component of one's internal perception. It also assesses one's propensity to remain self-directed and openly expressive of thoughts and feelings, while communicating these feelings in a constructive and socially acceptable way.

III. Interpersonal

Interpersonal is the third category in the EQ-i 2.0 Assessment. It is made up of three skills: Interpersonal relationships, empathy, and social responsibility. The category of interpersonal includes the ability to develop and maintain relationships based on trust and compassion, articulate an understanding of another's perspective, and act responsibly while showing concern for others, their team, or their greater community/organization.

IV. Decision-Making:

This fourth category is made up of the skills of problem-solving, reality testing, and impulse control. Decision-making involves the way in which one uses emotional information—how well one understands the impact emotions have on decision-making, including the ability to resist or delay impulses, remaining objective, which will aid in problem-solving.

V. Stress Management

Stress management is the fifth category. It is made up of the following skills: Flexibility, stress tolerance, and optimism. It involves how well one can cope with the emotions associated with change, and unfamiliar and unpredictable circumstances, while remaining hopeful about the future and being resilient in the face of setbacks and obstacles.

An indicator of emotional health and well-being is **HAPPINESS**. Happiness is not measured itself but is a combination of four of the EI skills. It is characterized by feelings of satisfaction, contentment, and the ability to enjoy the many aspects of one's life. The four skills most often associated with happiness are self-regard, optimism, interpersonal relationships, and self-actualization.

There are two of the MHS EQ-i 2.0 reports that are appropriate for youth, depending on their age and abilities. The EQ-i 2.0 Workplace Report is normed for adults, but also appropriate for older youth. It provides a detailed 21-page report with an individual's score within each of the 15 skills in comparison to others like you. The report then identifies areas of strengths and areas of growth, along with some specific suggestions on improving a specific skill, while pointing out how some of your higher and lower scores can impact each other. Each assessment completed is augmented with a feedback session with a qualified person certified in EQ-I 2.0. The EQ-i 2.0 Higher Ed Report is normed for college students and provides three reports: 1) A 10-page quick summary that is immediately available to the student who completed the assessment. This report provides limited feedback of the top three strengths and two areas for development which can be augmented with the feedback session; 2) A comprehensive report which is a 17-page report designed for only a qualified user and containing results and development strategies designed to assist the student in understanding the assessment results during a feedback session; and 3) An 18-page counselor report. This report contains results, responses and developmental strategies for all 15 skills and is only for a qualified user to offer assistance with interpretation of the report and to assist students in understanding the results and creating a development plan. This can also be utilized when the assessment is incorporated into a class or group in a high school or college.

EI & Application to Children

The following information on the chart below EI and Application to Children has been generously provided by and printed here with permission by and © Dr. Korrel Kanoy of Developmental Associates.[26]

EI and APPLICATION TO CHILDREN
I. Self-Perception Composite APPLICATION TO CHILDREN:
IMPORTANT CORRECTION! **Emotional Self-awareness:** Feelings that are recognized can be managed; understanding triggers allows children to respond with more reflection when an emotion is triggered. **Self-regard:** Self-criticism erodes confidence; lack of confidence hinders performance. Accurate awareness can help children leverage strengths and improve weaknesses.
Self-actualization: Children perform better with clear goals, a desire to achieve when they have passion for "work"; children need to explore lots of activities to find their own passions.
II. Self-Expression Composite APPLICATION TO CHILDREN:
Emotional self-expression: Children need to know how to effectively and appropriately express emotions so they can resolve situations that may detract from success or good relationships.
Assertiveness: A base level of assertiveness is necessary to approach a teacher for help, ward off a bully, or just to speak up in class.

26 www.developmentalassociates.com/about/korrelkanoy

Independence: Children need enough independence to separate effectively from parents, and function autonomously—but not so much they don't seek help when needed.

III. Interpersonal Composite APPLICATION TO CHILDREN

Interpersonal relationships: Making new friends, knowing how to connect with others and becoming integrated into social groups is part of well-being (too much can hinder academics).

Empathy: Getting along with others and being open to people different from yourself first requires a child to understand that person's perspective.

Social Responsibility: Children with developed social responsibility understand, accept and act upon their responsibility to the group (family, school, team, club or classmates).

IV. Decision-Making Composite APPLICATION TO CHILDREN

Reality Testing: Children with good reality testing skills can accurately judge academic (how long will my homework take?) and social (is this someone who might be a good friend?) situations.

Problem-Solving: Many children do not know a problem exists until it is too late to solve it effectively; knowing a problem exists and accurately assessing the cause is key to resolving it; avoiding problems doesn't make them go away.

Impulse Control: The ability to resist temptations (TV, social media, texts) protects a child from making poor choices that lead to greater stress; patience helps develop effective work habits.

V. Stress Management Composite APPLICATION TO CHILDREN
Stress Tolerance: Stress is created by both + and − events (tests, sports, activities, family life, etc.); if one is too reactive to stress, cognitive disorganization occurs and internal agitation can lead to dislike of school or other consequences.
Flexibility: Children must adapt to changes in environments whether it is differences in teaching styles, a parental divorce, change in schools, etc. Flexibility promotes successful adaptation.
Optimism: Optimism is predictive of multiple positive outcomes such as better health and more success. Kids face adversity and staying positive will support their success.
© Dr. Korrel Kanoy of Developmental Associates. Reprinted with permission.

Summary

Emotional intelligence is made up of everyday skills that we all have. These are skills that can be learned and developed. It is important to pay attention to how these skills interact with each other, and if some of them need further strengthening, as an imbalance of skills can create problems for us. Someone who has high scores in assertiveness and independence, yet low scores in empathy and impulse control would look and act like a bully. Different professions and different life skills may require one to draw on various combinations of these skills. When youth are encouraged to learn and practice EI skills, they often become happier, healthier, and more successful adults. (Successful in the way that they are better able to achieve success in academics, employment as well as in personal relationships.) Now, who wouldn't want that for themselves or for their children?

How does emotional intelligence fit into the Supportive Youth Coaching Model? It is part of the core methods. EI supports youth strengthening themselves, increasing skills as well as supporting their educational achievements. Adults who are familiar with and have developed EI skills can infuse this learning and EI practice into their work with youth, at home, in communities, or educational and therapeutic settings. Adults working with youth need to do their own work on EI, as they are models for the youth they are working to impact. Working on your own EI skills can support your effectiveness not only with youth but with your own professional goals as well. You can learn and practice these skills on your own or through an assessment, through coaching, or a formal program. Once you as an adult are familiar and comfortable with EI and its skills, you will be more able to work with youth on these skills successfully. You can't teach what you don't know, and youth will be the first to point out any discrepancies in your role modeling for them.

> **Emotional intelligence skills are super important for youth to learn and practice in order to function as healthy adults.**

In summary, emotional intelligence skills are super important for youth to learn and practice in order to function as healthy adults. It will support their success in academics, employment, and relationships. Our IQ might be what helps us qualify for higher education or employment at a specific job; however, it is our EQ (or EI) that will help us play well and do better. Adults in youth-work need to become aware of and build their own emotional intelligence so that they can best support youth in developing these skills. To paraphrase Daniel Goleman, in his book Emotional Intelligence, EQ can matter more than IQ (1995, page 228): "Why not do what we can to prevent the need for children to need psychotherapy to recover from emotional challenges, and give them the nurturing and guidance that cultivates the essential emotional skills needed to thrive?"

What is your take-away from this chapter?

What are the implications for your work with youth?

CHAPTER 10

MOVING YOU FORWARD

We've covered a lot here, yet we've barely begun. I've outlined for you why this book is important (Chapter 1), why life coaching for youth is important (Chapter 2), some of the basics about life coaching (Chapter 3), my dissertation research on coaching youth and the model I created called "A Supportive Youth Coaching Model" (Chapters 3 and 4), developmental issues in youth (Chapter 5), when to refer to a mental health professional (Chapter 6), ethical considerations in coaching minor youth (Chapter 7), core competencies (Chapter 8), and emotional intelligence in youth (Chapter 9). It's time to talk about what to do moving forward.

I created the Supportive Youth Coaching Model in combination from my own experience working with youth, from my coach training, and from my research with other certified youth coaches from around the world. It is meant to support both individual coaches and coach training organizations to provide appropriate and quality youth coaching. The model is written as a guide so that coaches or organizations can use it to create their own individualized programming or training. It is imperative that adults who work with youth are competent, ethical, and knowledgeable about their work and their client population. Ultimately, this is for the benefit and protection of youth.

By now I hope you've realized that coaching youth is an amazingly powerful way to support youth moving forward. Coaches don't try to motivate youth and get them to do something we want them to do. This motivational approach is all about helping youth tap into their own wisdom through exploration, learning, discovery, and setting goals that they really desire. This is how youth motivate themselves, and this is why life coaching is considered the latest motivational approach.

> It is imperative that adults who work with youth are competent, ethical, and knowledgeable about their work and their client population.

If you're interested in becoming a certified coach, there are many, many organizations worldwide that can assist you. If you're already a certified coach and want to receive further youth-specific training, there are a handful of coach training programs specifically focused on coaching children, teens, or young adults. However, these are changing and growing each year. I would recommend going through an accredited coach training organization, where you can assure your credentials will be valued.

What Do Youth Coaches Need?

My dissertation research surveyed youth coaches. They need (and want) to be successful. The following four areas were deemed most important: a) collaboration, b) supervision/mentoring, c) awareness and cooperation, and d) training. No one of us is an island, and youth coaching can be a very isolating experience if you are not connected to others doing similar work. It is important to connect with other youth coaches. Some of the coach training programs for youth have their own collaborative groups, and there are a few listed as well on both Facebook and LinkedIn. The former ICF youth coaches' group was moved over to LinkedIn and is (currently) a closed group that you can apply to be a member. It's called "Life Coaching Teens & Young Adults". It has grown from our 50 members to well over 3500. The current difficulty with this group is folks wanting to market themselves rather than collaborate, although we are working to change this. For those who are new to working with youth or new to coaching youth, there is a benefit to receiving supervision and/or mentoring from someone who has experience in youth coaching. Awareness and cooperation are needed from both coaching organizations as well as other youth-serving organizations as to what is youth coaching and how important it can be to support youth and assist them in being more successful in academics, employment, and in their relationships with others. Training is needed for coaches working with youth, especially in the area of a) coach training, b) adolescent development, c) ethics in working with minor youth, and d) group facilitation if you plan to do coaching of youth in groups.

Questions Matter

If you've picked up this book, then I'm guessing you have some interest in coaching youth. What better way than to end with some coaching questions either for yourself or for the youth with whom you work? If you do a web search on "coaching questions" you'll have immediate access to thousands of questions. There is no one right question. Not one question is better than another. The question that matters the most is the one that elicits thoughts and motivation towards action. The best way for that to happen is after some serious listening.

- What would you do if you knew you could not fail?

- What's stopping you?

- What will happen if you do nothing?

- What values of yours are inside this goal?

- Who in your circle can support you with this goal?

- What would bring your motivation from a 5 to an 8?

- If you could change just one thing in your life, what would it be?

- What question should I ask you?

- What questions should you ask yourself?

- What's something that you've always dreamed of doing?

- What's the worst that could happen?

- What's the best that could happen?

- What excuses do you tell yourself or others?

- What promises do you make to yourself?

- What brings you joy?

- What happened the last time you listened to yourself?

Action Plan Challenge

Now that you've read this book, in the spirit of coaching, I'd like to challenge you to take your insight or learning to the next level by completing the following action plan. After all, you've picked up this book for a reason. One of the best ways for you to learn a new way of goal setting is to practice it!

What is one idea or thought in this book that sparked your interest or is something you'd like to follow up on?

_____

_____

_____

Now create a SMART-VIEW goal (from Chapter 4) for yourself, based on that thought or idea.

Specific:

_____

_____

_____

Measurable:

_____

_____

_____

Action:

_____

_____

_____

Realistic:

_____

_____

_____

Time frame:

_____

_____

_____

Values:

_____

_____

_____

Importance:

_____

_____

_____

Evaluate:

_____

_____

_____

Who?

_____

_____

_____

On my website www.SandiLindgren.com (formerly www.isupportyouth.com) you will find some free resources that might also support youth, including The Supportive Youth Coaching Cheat-Sheet, an example of a coaching agreement for minor youth, a summary of the 15 emotional intelligent skills (from the EQ-i 2.0 assessment), and more. I will also be posting on my website any updates, groups and training opportunities.

My wish for you is that somewhere in this book you found an idea, a piece of inspiration, some knowledge or some support to help you moving forward in your work with youth. My wish for all youth is to be supported by healthy adults, who have their best interests in mind and professional adults who have the knowledge, skills, and abilities to support them in a way that brings out the best in them. With these in mind, we need to prioritize proactive rather than reactive support for youth. Children and youth need to become a priority in our world. We need to find a way to provide supportive opportunities for ALL youth to experience the power of coaching, preferably from someone who looks like them and has some similar or relatable generational experiences. Right now, youth coaching is most often experienced by upper class students who have affluent parents or schools that have the resources to hire coaches. The only way that will happen is for more adults to be trained in youth coaching, for more educational systems and youth-serving agencies to bring in professionally trained life coaches to work with youth, and for agencies to change the way the word "coaching" is used by more clearly defining the word coaching and hiring trained and certified life coaches to do the work.

It is my hope that this book will help fuel the fire for coaching youth to explode on a global level. Youth from all walks of life should get to experience the power or coaching! I plan to continue this work to support youth by supporting those adults and youth-serving organizations interested in the same. I wish you success in your endeavors.

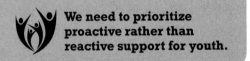

We need to prioritize proactive rather than reactive support for youth.

Sandi Lindgren, PhD, MSW
sandi@sandilindgren.com
612.598.0774

OTHER BOOKS RECOMMENDED BY BLACK CARD BOOKS

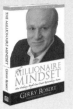

The Millionaire Mindset
How Ordinary People Can
Create Extraordinary Income
Gerry Robert
ISBN: 978-1-927411-00-1

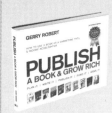

**Publish a Book &
Grow Rich**
How to Use a Book as
a Marketing Tool &
Income Accelerator
Gerry Robert
ISBN: 978-1-77204-546-8

Target Practice
8 Mistakes That Ruin a
Love of the Game
Chris Dyson
ISBN: 978-1-77204-459-1

Flight of Your Life
How to Get from Where You
Are to Where You Dream to Be
Theresa Barnabei
ISBN: 978-1-77204 -732-5

Eternal Optimism
How to Make Things Happen
James Baker, PhD
ISBN: 978-1-77371-222-2

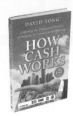

How Cash Works
Exploring the Unexpected
Benefits of Property
Investment in the New Age
David Tong
ISBN: 978-1-77204-895-7

Beautiful, Inside and Out
What You Ought to
Know about Autism
How to Embrace the Unique
Way Your Child Is Flourishing
Sazini Nzula, Ph
ISBN: 978-1-77204-982-4

Is Salary a Bribe?
Don't Forget Your Dreams
William Phua and
Christina Heng
ISBN: 978-1-77371-026-6

OTHER BOOKS RECOMMENDED BY BLACK CARD BOOKS

Multiply Your Coaching Business
10 New Marketing Realities for the Coaching & Consulting Industries
Gerry Robert and
Kevin Judge, CEC
ISBN: 978-1-77371-050-1

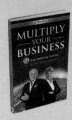

Multiply Your Business
10 New Marketing Realities for the Real Estate Industries
Gerry Robert &
Theresa Barnabei, DREC
ISBN: 978-1-77204-774-5

Hot Chixs Hot Sex
How to Survive Menopause
Irene Stronczak-Hogan
ISBN: 978-1-77204-059-3

Yes, You Can!
Your Roadmap To Dream, Create, and Profit
Virginia Phillips
ISBN: 978-1-77204-649-6

Reinvigorated Caregivers
7 Amazing Ways to Become Remarkable at Caring for People with Dementia
Naomi Dongelmans, MD
ISBN: 978-1-77204-107-1

Get Off the Cash Flow Roller Coaster!
A Real Estate Agent's Guide to Becoming a Money Magnet STOP Playing It Safe!
Amy Donaldson
ISBN: 978-1-77204-948-0

The Rod Effect
Master 8 Philosophies That Took Me from the Projects to NFL SUPER BOWL STARDOM
Rod Smith
ISBN: 978-1-77204-254-2

Baby Boomer Bonding
Luxurious and Meaningful Lifestyle without Breaking the Bank
Anne Marie Cummings
ISBN: 978-1-77204-996-1

www.blackcardbooks.com